Wine Maniacs

Life in the Wine Biz

By

Layne V. Witherell

CONTENTS

Wine Maniacs

I don't go to wine tastings much anymore. The little wine wonk wannabes parading around remind me too much of me thirty years ago. They are doing their damnedest to somehow fake their way into the wine biz, holding their glasses just so while reciting the obligatory and meaningless mantras on the wine de jour's bouquet, it's oh so special toasted oak, those notes of beets and a hint of road tar and the rest of those lies that emerge from their teeming little minds.

As complex as all of this seems, the wine biz, when you actually manage to fake your way in, is pretty simple and can be boiled down to being the domain of four personality types.

<u>The Wine Maniac:</u> This is what all of those wannabes strive to become, a living, breathing vintage chart. Wine maniacs are constantly in search of every new and obscure wine, along with it's descriptor of the moment. They try to stay one step ahead of that soon to become rare bottle that has recently been hyped by the press, or what's worse, the completely over hyped and irresistible vintage of the century.

Unfortunately, our per capita consumption is not much higher than the country of Latvia so the wine maniac is often disappointed by the average person's total lack of interest in their newfound passion. This is possibly the reason that wine maniacs travel exclusively in small packs, and regard what they are doing so seriously.

The Amateur: This is usually a winery owner. They are the wine maniac cubed, and have piles of money made by doing something else. The old truism is that they will need those excess millions when their wine venture goes belly up, and it usually does. They are a great adventure for a serious student of the subject as they are an easy person to spot, and fun to watch during their ascent and descent.

Also, those new little wannabes turned reps can qualify as amateurs; if only they can cling to their tasting glasses and hype filled notes long enough to make it through several pay checks. Note: they are not as dangerous to themselves as the amateur winery owner.

The Nepotist: Usually small, family owned businesses breed that peculiar trait called nepotism. The wine biz is a continual breeding ground for this type. Watch for "Junior" spending his entire career being a mindless nuisance, usually at your expense .If you are thinking about joining wine mania, then you will no doubt encounter one or more of these types- unfortunately as your boss.

The Guru: A form of wine saint that every maniac aspires to become and a very few succeed. This is a person enthralled in a lifetime of tasting and seriously thinking about the stuff. Just put on your saffron robe, sit down and shut up, and take a good set of notes.

The wine biz is a magnet for the flamboyant, the eccentric and a flock of ego driven types. This book is a chronicle of my adventures in this highly erratic world. It is chronological, and the stories tell things as they happened. And along the way we might learn a little something.

So, why me? In 25 plus years I have been a wholesaler (both rep and management), a retail buyer, an importer, radio talk show host, wine journalist, wine competition judge and taught over 15 years of wine classes. This book is part memoir and part "how to". At the end of the day, it is still a romp through Wine Mania.

California Rising:

"The Day California Shook the World"– Frank Prial

In the early '70s, I walked to work every morning enveloped in the smells of roasting espresso beans and sizzling pans of garlic wafting from Italian restaurants. I lived in bohemian North Beach in San Francisco. My apartment was at the very top of Telegraph Hill; a tiny three-room garret that let in just enough light, at certain times of the day, to make one appreciate the expectations worshipers felt at Stonehenge's every solstice.

The major advantage for an adventurous college student like me was that I could experience the endless parade of fascinating characters that made North Beach bigger than life. There were the remaining beats, still assembled in basic black for reunion poetry readings. North Beach was their original haunt, and the beats were accorded special status when they arrived for reunions at City Lights Bookstore, the scene of their early literary triumphs.

Second in the triumvirate of North Beach life were the hippies. They had passed their cultural peak a few years back, and many of their tribe members had already returned home to Kansas. Nonetheless, it took but a few to make a bold color statement. The hippies' San Francisco territory was staked out in the Haight-Ashbury, so North Beach locals regarded them as tourists.

The most recent group to arrive on the scene was the punks. Several local Filipino restaurant owners hosted their raucous concerts. The punks ironically dressed like the beats, but were younger, wilder and hateful. They were anarchists playing musical instruments as weapons.

These divergent groups would converge only at the world's most cavernous shack: Mike's Pool Hall on Broadway. Smack in the middle of everybody's haunts, Mike's resembled a relic from the old Barbary Coast days of San Francisco. You are sitting at the bar, eating pasta and drinking beer, and WHOOSH! a trap door opens and the next thing you know you're a mess cook on a tramp steamer headed to Shanghai. All you could see in the galley were grungy black berets, outrageous tie-dyes, and black T-shirts screaming Sid Vicious slogans in white letters.

Mike's eventually closed and was replaced by a family styled restaurant whose motto was "Rain or shine, there's always a line." Frankly, "Rain or shine, there's always Shanghai" had a better edge.

My choice in colleges was a philosophical extension of life in North Beach. San Francisco State University was miles away from North Beach, but very close to its bohemian spirit. Famed local artists studied there, and the beats introduced their work at seminars they taught there during the 1950s. The faculty taught with passion, and implored their students to make their avocations into their vocations. In other words, do what you love.

In another quarter there was a large degree of newfound passion. The wine scene in San Francisco was electric. Large numbers of locals had traveled to Europe to discover life beyond Wonder Bread and Coca-cola. Reasonably priced, high-quality French wines were selling in the stores on Solano Avenue, a popular shopping venue in Berkeley for those just back from Europe. New California releases were found at stores in the city, an area that had always housed California wine bottling facilities and their distribution warehouses. Oakland, always funky and third-world, provided wines from little-known regions like Algeria, which was always a godsend to those on a student's budget.

Purchasing a few well-worn wine books and relying on the guidance of local wine merchants helped decipher European wine labels. Figuring out those unknown places and unknown grapes, together with all-important vintages, would land you a better-than-decent wine for the money, and a great experience to boot.

I found from the beginning of my wine quest that the best merchants were always opinionated and passionate, not so much over what they personally drank but where the best values, vintages and qualities lie. Roger had a hip Solano Avenue store, with its inlaid wood and rough hewn floors and cabinets. The store was scattered with wines of his own selection and passion.

Each week, Roger had one region he would promote, and another he would violently lay into. Bordeaux was the object of this week's wrath. "They are expensive, and made and sold by arrogant, greedy bastards." Now that's what I called a wine merchant telling it like it is. About a month later, Roger's promotion for the week was Bordeaux. How strange is that?

According to my wine man, Bordeaux was in the throws of a major scandal, called ironically Winegate. Due to the popularity of Bordeaux in the early '70s, there wasn't enough wine to meet demand —especially given that the value of French wine is based on a strict hierarchical system of wine regions. By law, the wine's birthplace must appear on every label.

Enter Pierre Bert —short and dapper, with an outsized nose and large, black horn-rimmed glasses, topped off by a snappy Sinatra-style hat. He is, aside from being a Bordeaux wine merchant, a shady character. Bert devised an ingenious scheme of taking the paperwork from white Bordeaux wine (not sought after at the time), changing a few words, and substituting it for the prized red Bordeaux. Change a few words and make a fortune. Meanwhile, the white wine was dumped, and the red wine being billed as Bordeaux was coming from a region much lower in the food chain.

With Bordeaux prices plummeting and wine people panicking, what really made the scandal were the little things, such as the rumored signs on stacks of wine in Bordeaux producers' cellars that read, "For sale in America only." The piece de resistance was indicted co-conspirator No. 2 Lionel Cruse claiming he was completely innocent, just like President Nixon in Watergate.

My wine merchant was suddenly big on Bordeaux because the real stuff—the honest stuff—was coming in at wine scandal panic prices. His recommended wine of the week was the 1955 Chateau La Mission Haut Brion, one of the finest wines in Bordeaux and my first taste of great wine.

Great wines light up the entire dining room. Since I lived in the garret, this one at least lit up the entire kitchen table. Just smelling that wine was surreal, like sticking your head into a cedar cigar box filled with blackberry essence and the most marvelous ancient rocks.

Poor Roger went out of business. Having learned about, tasted and bought wines for a couple of years, I thought it would be interesting to dip my toes into the biz. Taking a part-time buying job in a wine shop on Solano Avenue brought me my first guru: James Arthur Field. He was lean and lanky, dressed in faded, pressed Levi's jeans and a Levi's shirt. His ride was a 1959 Cadillac with the trunk cut out to hold a cargo of James Arthur Field White and Red in half-gallon bottles. A Dartmouth alum, James Arthur was an advertising exec taking early retirement in order to perfect his true calling: the making and blending of the world's finest jug table wine.

Hanging around with James Arthur was like hanging around a George Plimpton styled rodeo cowboy with a Harvard education lurking in his past. During those days, the typical California Chablis or Burgundy was a generic no-place-of-origin wine made from over-produced, nondescript grapes that rendered little more than a thin, bland drink.

James Arthur became the Ben and Jerry of California jug wine, blending a variety of grapes and styles to produce everyday tipple that was truly exciting. Each week, we would unload cases from his Caddie, piling his elegant, yet understatedly labeled, bottles in the shop. One week later, they were all gone.

What elevated James Arthur from pure maniac or even amateur was that he could stick his nose into any glass and tell you the wine's origin, birth date and pedigree. Every time he appeared in the store, our glasses came out, the notebooks fell open and we were ready for a tutorial. He gladly suffered our rookie questions with patience and understanding.

California wines were coming on, but one really had to work to find the best stuff. The mahogany paneled stores in the city would periodically have Stony Hill and Hanzell chardonnays, which were as good as their French counterparts. They weren't just something to quaff with pasta or ribs.

These new California wines were startlingly different. Stony Hill chardonnay delivered a distinct flavor we hadn't tasted in California: the taste of power and earth. Drinking members of this fresh generation of wines such as David Bruce Zinfandel, Mondavi Fume Blanc and Grand Cru Vineyards Gewurztraminer became a religious experience.

The road trip was another important path in discovering the California wine scene. Any funky guide books whose title contained the words "Little" or "Hidden" were the best because the writers weren't kidding, this stuff was off the beaten path.

On the road, we sought the authentic breed, the old timers, or as James Arthur called them, "the deliberate peasants." Frank Nervo, a true maniac, had a shabby little winery on Redwood Highway near Geyserville. Once you entered his winery, you were entirely in his world. It was like a serious budget trip to the outer reaches of Europe. We tasted wine in old tumblers as Frank, dressed in bib overalls; brow beat us through several Zinfandels, a Pinot St. George, and his mysterious Beclan Cabernet (the few remaining acres were ripped up several years later). We were there for his $2.50 zinfandel. Five years old, this one was to be our weekend wine, and by far our best find for the money.

One Saturday morning, while on a Zin run, we noticed a well-appointed Lincoln in Frank's parking lot. This was not the type of vehicle you usually saw at the Nervo Winery. Frank was hauling a case to the trunk, when he swore, "Didn't even taste the wine and he bought it!"

We followed him into the tasting room where he promptly found and opened a bottle. As we tasted the wine in a state of awe, Frank smiled. "That is my 1944 zinfandel that he just bought." We didn't have enough money to buy a case, but we had enough for a few precious bottles to go with the barbequed goat, a favorite Italian North Beach specialty served in the North Beach garret.

Sadly, the highway department chopped through Frank's vineyard to add another lane for progress, and Geyser Peak Winery bought what was left to put up its tasting room. Much as we looked, we could find no zinfandel to replace Frank's. In his wisdom, James Arthur suggested we visit Amador County, about 150 miles away, to check out their zin.

We began at the tiny, vernacular town of Sutter Creek. Untouched by modern civilization, this unique spot was the 19th century gold-mining mother lode. Today, Sutter Creek hosts more bed and breakfasts, but that is about it for change.

When we visited, the town's center of activity was a yard sale at the Trinity Episcopal Church. Standing in front of a table full of just-published wine books was vicar of the parish Rev. E. Frank Henriques, renaissance wine guru, author of those books, and seer of all things local. He was a "Roman Retread" —a priest who married a nun and decided to call Sutter Creek home. In his spare time he ran the local wine shop.

Henriques was dressed in his head-to-toe black garb and white collar, even while running the deli and making you a sandwich. To the uninitiated, it was a fairly unnerving sight. His shop was small and cluttered, with wines sticking out of unlikely nooks. We tasted through a few of his scarce German Rieslings and headed out to visit more wineries.

We found the D'Agostini Winery and Story Vineyard the most interesting, and soon realized that this place produced vastly different grapes than Sonoma County. Amador Zin was pruny, peppery, intense, and loaded with natural alcohol. Amador vines were ancient because few people bothered to replant or change anything. By the time people discovered these gems, there was no reason to alter the vineyards. Also, because Amador is farther inland than Sonoma, the region is hotter and the zinfandel grapes riper. These early Amador zins were wines to have instead of a meal, not alongside one. We hauled a few cases back to San Francisco just for fun.

After following great advice from James Arthur, I sought advice from other readily-accessible gurus. The major wine bible of the day was Leon Adams' Wines of America, a treasure trove containing most of the known wisdom on American wines. The best thing of all was that Mr. Adams was in the phone book.

"Come on in. Make yourself at home. Find a place to sit." Adams office was crammed to overflowing with books and ancient filing cabinets, a testament to a lifetime of collecting and accumulating information. Adams had that 1940s journalist look about him with his tweed jacket, large-framed glasses and pipe that never seemed to stay lit. We talked about early Napa, forgotten grapes, upcoming wineries and existing pioneers. "You need to go and see Frank Bartholomew, he'll set you straight," Adams directed.

As it turned out, Frank Bartholomew was one of the strangest California maniac wine people I encountered. In the 1940s, Bartholomew bought the Buena Vista Winery in Sonoma at auction —sight unseen —as basically a place to build a summer house. The buildings were ramshackle and the locals had little memory of the estate's original operation. Bartholomew, with Adams' help, researched the estate and discovered its historical significance.

Buena Vista was the winery built by California's "Father of Wine" Agoston Haraszthy. Haraszthy is one of those founders who truly fit the term "father," especially through his archetypal steps to becoming a successful businessman / guru in California. He arrived from a foreign country (Hungary), from an undivulged, mysterious past (Colonel? Count?). He viewed California as a giant opportunity (taking complete advantage of the situation). He became involved in the federal government as the head of the mint, was later indicted and proven innocent of stealing gold. He went into an emerging field (wine) and built a grand estate (a Pompeian villa no less). He went broke and tried to re-coup his losses by going to South America where he was eaten by alligators. Is this not the California story?

Haraszthy's major success was, however, his ability to convince everyone he met that one day soon California would become the greatest wine region in the world. Frank Bartholomew's little summer place turned into the rebuilding of a winery, cellar and original hand-dug tunnels —a restoration that was years in the making. Bartholomew may have been an amateur when he started, but he built the winery to national esteem, won a ton of medals in local competitions, and went off to build a neighboring winery called Hacienda.

The day I sat down to talk with Bartholomew, we retraced Heraszthy's career footsteps through vineyards, winery and hand dug caves. Bartholomew was clearly distracted He had retired as chairman of the board of United Press International and was musing about writing his memoirs. As he sat ramrod straight, complete with eye patch and Hathaway shirt, I could tell this was a man who had something on his mind and did not take no for an answer.

Bartholomew then quietly divulged an unpublished memoir story. At the end of World War II, he was granted an exclusive interview with captured Japanese Prime Minister Tojo, the man who launched the attack on Pearl Harbor. During the interview, Tojo pulled a smuggled revolver from under his jacket and tried to shoot himself. Bartholomew and the guards disarmed him and saved his life. Tojo was tried as a war criminal and hanged several years later. There was a crackle of excitement in the air as I drove off. Between Haraszthy and Bartholomew, there was no doubt that California earned its well deserved reputation for local eccentricity.

In my quest to seek out more characters in the wine biz, I discovered that road trips didn't have to be long to be interesting. The name "Cakebread" kept coming up, but no one could identify his whereabouts. I found his address in the Oakland phone directory under "Cakebread Automotive." A drive to East Oakland to meet him resembled an outing to meet the Hells Angels or Black Panthers.

Jack Cakebread sat in his glassed-in office, surrounded by brake jobs and pulled transmissions. His vision of founding a Napa winery was displayed in the myriad vineyard maps plastered around his cramped office. He figured it was just a matter of selling the auto business and turning it into some Napa Cabernet and Chardonnay. That was a proper maniac: to have the ability to predict the future of wine while surrounded by motor oil.

Soon after my meeting with Cakebread, I began to see concrete changes in the future of wine soon when I took another improbable part-time wine job as an assistant sommelier in one of San Francisco's top restaurants.

A lowly junior assistant, I was stuck in the far back dining room, where the only sounds you are certain of hearing are the opening and closing of the kitchen and bathroom doors. You get the customers who don't dine out often, or those who don't think of lavishly tipping the maitre'd. Ironically, in either case they usually don't realize they are in a less-than-attractive location. Most are simply thrilled to be going out at all.

The best thing about my job as an assistant was pulling corks from half-bottles of Mateus Crackling Rose. My most glorious moment came during a packed New Year's Eve when four tipsy women sat down and ordered a bottle of Champagne. At the height of the rush, the cork blew, spraying all four literally from head to toe. I calmed a bit and graciously poured the remaining Champagne into their glasses. They all looked up, somewhat dazed, thinking it was part of a show, and gave me a round of applause, and, I might add, a generous tip. Management was not so generous.

On a sidenote, looking back at the hierarchy of wine on this mid-'70s list is intriguing: France has 107 wines, Germany has 31, and California a mere 50. Today's version would have 157 California wines, with the rest divided among a dozen countries.

After this part-time job taught me that all it took to be granted a great table was a folded $50 bill slipped to the greased palm of the maitre'd, it was difficult going out to a nice restaurant and keep a straight face. However, I did up one evening in late May 1976 at a favorite chop house, ready to order one of their great Bordeaux. Sorry, it was out. In its place, the waiter recommended a 1973 Cabernet Sauvignon from a new winery called Stag's Leap. Why not? It was only $10.

I did the swirling, sniffing and preliminary sip and sat there speechless. After a few years of tasting and studying wine, this is what you dream will happen: the great ringer lands in your glass, and you know it. It was big-time Bordeaux flavor writ large in California wine. It was new, unique, and fabulous.

The next day, the San Francisco Chronicle's front-page headline whooped that an unknown California winery had bested the finest French wines in a Paris competition with French judges. It was proclaimed the finest wine in the world. That little Stag's Leap Cabernet climbed to $150 in the same restaurant, and disappeared in minutes.

The event was called "The Day California Shook the World" and "The Judgment of Paris." There was an unbelievable feeling of wine mania in the air. It was a great day to go into the wine biz.

Early Oregon

"Touring Oregon's wine district today is what it must have been to roam through California's Napa Valley back around the turn of the century."
Tom Stockley, 1977

The Oregon experience began with a phone call from a friend in Portland, tipping me off about an ad in the local paper for a sales rep. The job was with a small family-run wholesaler headed by Ken —a middle-aged blustery type who favored a Beatle haircut, turtlenecks and one huge, expensive piece of Indian jewelry. His scatter-brained wife, whom I nicknamed Pocahontas, fancied herself an Indian princess. Dressed in her requisite buckskin, she wore more turquoise than any slightly built make-believe Indian could carry. Their daughter Jessie, cute and willowy, was just along for the nepotistic ride.

They were amateur, amateur and amateur. The first clue came when they talked incessantly about how much they liked "all those wines they had in Europe," and complained about how they just couldn't find them here. Can you say, "Open your wallet please?"

My boss, the lovely young Jess, was both an amateur and a nepotist — not a particularly thrilling combo. Her executive decisions included inviting a notorious food critic to our cozy warehouse/tasting room combo: Matt Kramer, the new Willammette Week magazine's restaurant reviewer who was ripping the town's dining scene apart with his razor-edged ranting. The most sacrosanct of establishments were laid naked and bare, leading a local wine rep to call Kramer "Mattie the K" —a little play on the boisterous deejay from the '50s. Coming from Chicago, Kramer landed on Portland like an elephant come to slice and dice the locals, all for a whopping $25 a week. Local legend had it that Mom handed him a pile of stock coupons and pointed him west.

Surprisingly, Kramer turned out to be a balding young man with a slight build. Unsurprisingly, he was also the most opinionated and not-afraid-to-blurt-it-out person I ever encountered. He knew nothing about wine, but his supple mind made up for the lack of experience. He later would end up being one of the rare people to go from nepotist to amateur to maniac to guru, eventually writing some of the most insightful wine thoughts between two covers in the last 20 years of the 20th century. Who knew?

Unfortunately, nothing came of our little tasting with Jessie. That was a shame, because without any pull from the press, I got to be the one who endowed the wines with their 15 minutes of fame. I did this by simply climbing into the old Chrysler wagon and making the requisite 15-plus sales calls a day.

This required a properly equipped salesman's vehicle. Two cups of coffee of indeterminate age in the front cup-holders were flanked by the endless pile of laundry in the front seat, garnished with a couple of maps. Those all-important account lists lie scattered on the floor. Riding in the rear seat were boxes filled with wine samples; and the scene was completed with piles of new restaurant license applications. That car was a rolling fortress. Add a bit of sheer willpower, and the wines would sell.

An axiom in sales is that 20 percent of your accounts will produce 80 percent of your revenue, and 20 percent of all reps make 80 percent of the money. With that in mind, the cleanliness of your ride accounts for zip. Your objective is to grab your stuff fast and hit those accounts.

What I had to work with was fairly backward compared to San Fransico. Portland in the late '70s was still light-blue collar as the high-tech industry began making inroads. Given the rapidly expanding 'burbs, real-estate agents and developers could manage to kill the occasional $200 bottle of Chateau Lafite with their salad course and feel little economic pain. The ethereal, delicate fruit of the wine would be immediately paralyzed by the vinaigrette salad dressing, but what the hell, a little glassful to celebrate the building of the latest strip mall.

One of the most important parts of sales is developing a nose for places destined to become the newest hot spots. I found a small underground restaurant in Old Town Portland that smelled like burgeoning success. Old Town was the 19th-century brick and stone remembrance of the city's seafaring past. As small businesses rapidly displaced what had become skid row, the area bloomed with life —one block and one building at a time.

Samples are a rep's magnet, and I opened almost every bottle in my car for the owner of this new hot spot. I explained to the wily little restaurant newcomer the glories of chardonnay, red Burgundy and German riesling. I went into which wine goes with which dish, how to serve the wines — basically, the A-to-Z of wines for the small restaurant.

Come restaurant opening time, I still had no wine order, so I decided to drop in under the guise of a civilian there for lunch. There they were, lining the back of the bar: my opened samples from several weeks' worth of visits.

A few bites of lunch and a glass of wine killed my hunch of the restaurant's pending success: the food was awful and the wine was shot.

Every bottle on the bar was undrinkable, having been opened for weeks. Oxygen is a wine assassin, and these should have been long buried. In the case of this hot little restaurant, there were no fresh samples for sale.

Fortunately, he didn't stay open long. Besides, there was an endless stream of these "hot new restaurants" opening, usually backed by an amateur's money and run by enough maniacs to guarantee at least a short term return for the money. I spent my days frantically proposing wine lists, putting together wine-by-the-glass programs for menus, and conducting wait staff trainings —all at breakneck speed.

I had just completed a proposed list for a new intriguing little place called Zorba the Buddha. It was owned and operated by the followers of the Bhaguan Sri Rashnish, a mystical Indian guru with a large "family" headquartered on a ranch in eastern Oregon.

The restaurant staff assembled for their training session dressed in robes, pants and shirts in shades of red and pink; the colors of the faithful. Locals harbored more than a little skepticism of their cult-like ways, their excessive hedonism, and the money they lavished on the Bhaguan himself. Did he really need all those Rolls Royces?

Ironically, regardless of their flowing attire, these people were articulate, professional, yuppie types who had, for one reason or another, decided to bag it all and wait tables in a cheesy little pseudo Indian restaurant in Portland. Here they were, working 18 to 20 hours a day for the greater glory of some long-bearded yogi —but who am I to judge?

I step up to the stage to demonstrate the opening and pouring of wine and explain the overall wine-and-food pairing shtick. All the staffers had their regulation 1.5 ounces of wine, and we were settling in to talk about the niceties and nuances of the subject, when all hell began to break loose.

Between the raucous talking, loud laughter, and general groping fest, I realized that these people were all wrecked.

I was trying to be cool in the midst of this tableside show, but the more I talked about the glories of the wine list, the lower they slinked under their tables. As I finished my little spiel, the room turned into a sea of arms, legs and tongues. Bye folks. It was fun.

It didn't take me long to get it. I stood in the parking lot, wondering what had happened. No one gets that plastered on 1.5 ounces of wine, especially a group of 30-somethings, magenta robes and all. It must be their diet. Dr. Bhaguan's mind-control diet could have been the topic of someone's PhD thesis on cult nutrition.

The entire group eventually left town, and the Bhaguan fled to India. I'm sure that somewhere in eastern Oregon there is some old dude still driving a beat up magenta Rolls Royce.

Another restaurant show came when a rep from one of the wineries whose wines I sold called me breathlessly from California, asking to come up and present the next great wine —the one we couldn't live without in the market.

This winery was clever. Their marketing ploy was shrinking the front label with all of its mandated information so it resembled a typical small back label and sand blasting a slick design on the reverse side, turning the back of the bottle into the front. The first true American designer wine bottle. Hopefully, as with all designer goods, it would serve its purpose of inflaming the buying passions of all who encountered it.

At any rate, the restaurant we settled on for the presentation was wild with noise. I call these events"the chumps' night out," namely because you can't concentrate on scrutinizing the wine and thus wind up buying a dud.

As we prepared to leave, the couple at the next table engaged in a heated argument. She jumped up, knocking over a garish Gucci bag, spilling its contents all over the floor: 10,000 pills in all sizes, shapes and colors. Needless to say, the hot new brand we tasted that night didn't last long, and neither did the "hot" new restaurant.

The most interesting restaurant in town was a place called L'Omelette, a cool French bistro with an open-demonstration kitchen, a novel act for Portland. Complete with a formidable wine list, the establishment was headed by a man resembling an Iraqi rug merchant named David Adelsheim. With his heavy jowls and scruffy beard, Addelsheim gleefully tore into my list of French Burgundy, taking them apart as one would a recipe. He was experimenting with making pinot noir and chardonnay in his spare time, and tasting extensively to see what made Burgundy tick. Barrels, regions, vineyards —nothing survived his scrutiny.

Adelsheim's enduring claim to fame was the astute observation that Oregon would never rival California in wine volume. Even during the best of years, the state simply didn't have enough potential vineyard sites to effectively compete with its neighbor. With that in mind, Adelsheim convinced the band of struggling local wineries to enact tough laws regulating Oregon wine labels. There would be no oceans of bulk juice trucked across the border to be bottled and sold under the guise of "local wine" in this state. The place of origin listed on an Oregon wine label would mean something.

Traveling about, and getting a sense of the land, I caught glimpses of these small, local wineries and heard pieces of bios on the people who owned them. The most amazing thing to me about the early Oregon winery scene was that these people were from California, leaving careers in technology to settle in wine wilderness. Of course, to get to there they had to pass all the "Don't Californicate Oregon" signs and bumper stickers.

Eventually, I ventured into touring local wineries on weekends, meeting the winemakers to discover what Oregon had in store. To begin with, the climate here was cooler and wetter than California. We wouldn't be experiencing any great cabernet in this part of the world. It looked more like a struggle to the death between riesling, chardonnay, pinot noir, and the local crop of choice: the filbert nut.

The California transplant winemakers were not only in the process of reinventing themselves from city people to farmers, but they were also busy converting the Oregon farmland from filbert orchards to handkerchief-sized vineyards. Riesling was the most developed of grapes in Oregon, with chardonnay a far second. Pinot noir varied from downright wonderful to god-awful. Even so, there was no telling who was going to win: the grapes or the filberts. The limited number of wine drinkers in Portland would decide.

I began my explorations armed with Tom Stockley's pamphlet The Winery Trails of the Pacific Northwest. Eyrie Vineyards in McMinnville was open to tours twice a year for their chomping-at-the-bit, mailing-list maniac customers. Standing in this nondescript ex-turkey processing plant didn't give one a feeling of forthcoming gastronomic success. Winemaker Dave Lett hovered about, seeming more like a philosopher —or even a local filbert farmer —with his full beard and head-to-toe Pendleton attire. The pinot noir was excellent, the chardonnay good and the Oregon Spring Wine (a blend of pinot blanc and muscat ottonel) refreshing.

Amity Vineyards employed the only winemaker in Oregon not interested in reinventing himself. Myron Redford was straight off a Grateful

Dead tour bus, and he loved making wine. His winery resembled the backseat of my car —same size and definitely the same amount of confusion. His Pinot Noir Nouveau was marching to the beat of a different drummer. It had more in common with tofu and a side of sprouts than as an accompaniment for haute cuisine. Myron's work was, if nothing else, exciting.

Ponzi Vineyards in Beaverton was literally a garage operation. This would change with the upcoming new winery, though even the new space was small. Ponzi, an engineer by profession, designed rides for Disneyland before creating his own 10-acre agricultural kingdom. Ponzi's delicious pinot noir reigned supreme, along with his riesling, while his Oregon Harvest blended wine came in second place for its picnic-wine flavor profile.

Touring the Charles Coury Vineyards in Forest Grove was like wandering around the grounds of a circus. If Dave Lett was reticent, then Charles Coury was practically out in the parking lot forming his own drum corps. Even at rest he had a dynamic energy. The local press couldn't get enough of Charles Coury, and he looked the part as well. The khakis and blue chambray shirt are stained with an unknown multitude of grapes. The look is intense, complete with a thick semi-walrus mustache and monkish tonsure. The thumb placed thoughtfully on the chin with the last remnants of a cigarette being held by a thoroughly calloused wine stained hand. This guy, in a little known wine region, is serious.

First, his winery was the only one in the region with a true historical background. Wine Hill, complete with a 100-year-old farmhouse, had won a silver medal for its riesling at the 1904 St. Louis Worlds Fair. The estate was in derelict condition when Coury bought it.

Coury touted riesling, gewurztraminer and sylvaner. With his highly modern stainless steel equipment, Coury had plans. He had the option of purchasing additional land as well as grapes and juice from Washington State allowing him the ability to produce 200,000 gallons per year of German- and Alsatian-style wines. The wines were easy to drink and uncomplicated. It was a completely different concept from the Burgundian wines of Eyrie and Ponzi.

Oak Knoll in Hillsboro was the last stop on the tour. Winemaker Ron Vuylsteke, a short wizened local in a mechanic's jumpsuit, was in the tasting room sampling a few of his experiments. A native Oregonian, he too was reinventing himself. Until recently, the winery had produced mainly fruit wines (Oregon is renowned for its fruit), but he saw the shift toward table wines. Maybe it was all of those Californians moving in.

Vuylsteke was working with a variety of grapes and wine styles, trying to figure out what would grow best and what would be the wine that defined Oregon. We took the experiments into the house and had a long chat about where Oregon wines might be going. This was an honest and brilliant guy who was asking all the right questions. Two weeks later, I was sales manager of Oak Knoll.

Oak Knoll's hometown of Hillsboro was a funky little town lacking in amenities. The winery crew met every afternoon just down the road at the house of one of the part-timers. The place was an older country shack. The kitchen had a large woodstove and the adjoining living room and dining room were converted into one space, filled with a huge pool table.

Underneath the house was a basement setup that sucked the entire Hillsboro power supply dry: a forest of well-groomed and very content Sensemilla pot plants. The only problem in indulging would have been in getting home, since the half-hour commute over the mountain would turn into two hours. So much for the Sensemilla, I went home.

Oregon wines were virtually unknown outside their cramped tasting rooms, and it was time to jump back into the car and change some minds. I was given the requisite company car and an invaluable asset: a say in how the wines of Oak Knoll were made, which in turn meant the ability to shape the direction of Oregon wine.

I embarked on a continuous road show of tasting Oak Knoll wines alongside local food. After several years of slogging through the trenches, my breakthrough came when I convinced Jake's Famous Crawfish, a famed local restaurant, to put table tents touting Oregon wines on each table in their dining rooms. Jake's was best known for its fresh, skillfully prepared seafood.

The public took to it immediately, especially with the restaurant's staff talking up the wine and pairing it with food. It was no time before other restaurants followed suit. People began to prefer local pinot noir with fresh salmon over Chateau Lafite Rothschild destroyed by vinaigrette.

While getting recognition for the wine in restaurants was going well, the battle for retail store space was a lot tougher. Oregon wines, if they existed at all, lived on the bottom shelves. Oak Knoll wines were distributed by a local, yet formidable, powerhouse company. But for a small Oregon Winery, the head of the company was all but unapproachable.

Al C. Guisti was called The Godfather, and he was aptly named. One phonecall and your brand would rise to fame or sink to oblivion on the grocery store shelves in the market.

We met with Guisti one Saturday morning in his office. The scene resembled that of petitioners awaiting an audience with the tribal chieftain. I had been raising Cain with Guisti's lieutenants about our shabby placements, especially in lieu of the restaurant successes, and was nervous that The Godfather would give me a peck on the cheek and I would plunge through a trapdoor and never be seen again.

When he entered the room, my eyes bugged out. Marlon Brando should have been a double for Al C. Guisti. There he sat, bigger than life, wearing an old cardigan sweater and speaking with the sound of a shovel passing through a sidewalk full of gravel. I barely opened my mouth when he asked if I had seen the faded, painted sign on the back of his warehouse: "The New Italian Wine Company."

"My dad used to bring tank cars up from California after prohibition and we kids would work on the bottling line," he said. "That is how I got my start in the business." We talked about the early days of wine both during and after Prohibition.

As I got up to leave he slowly raised his hand and said, "Don't worry. If you think those wines will sell, that matter has been taken care of." It was the most miraculous two-shelf upward leap in the history of regional wines.

I found out later that Guisti had been reminiscing for good reason. He was dying of cancer, and the enforcement arm of the Oregon Liquor Control Commission was breathing down his neck. Seems the Safeway buyer who earned $12,000 per year had just gone out and bought a new Porsche and a condo on the coast. Since he wasn't in any family members' wills, the commission traced his new-found wealth back to Guisti. Guisti was fined and reprimanded, and the wine buyer wound up running the family shoe repair shop in South Dakota.

On the winery end, the riesling/pinot noir battle was still raging when suddenly the Charles Coury winery went out of business. Even with all that press: Poof! The question now was would someone assume the riesling banner as Coury had done so convincingly, or would pinot noir or chardonnay win the game?

My next trip to southern Oregon to see our distributor left me time for a couple of winery visits. I had heard tales of a riesling grown by Hillcrest Vineyard, an early '60s pioneer winery located in Roseburg, the heart of logging country.

The nature of the logging economy was that it was either boom or bust. Richard Sommer, founder, winemaker and caretaker, was a quiet, small-built man who wore a black beret. Picture a beatnik driving a tractor. The advantage the winery had with being in southern Oregon was its ability to ripen more grape varieties than the typical Oregon grower. Sommer had produced 14 wines, ranging from a superb riesling to cabernet to zinfandel. The thing that struck me about Sommer is that he chose and enjoyed his quirky, risky lifestyle, preferring to be a pioneer in Oregon than a teacher in California. Maybe Sommer was the last true beatnik.

If Richard Sommer was about lifestyle, then Siskiyou Vineyards was the edge. I was eager to try their cabernet, which I couldn't obtain in theWillamette Valley. Siskiyou must have been what Myron Redford of Amity secretly dreamed about. It was a fleet of Grateful Dead busses roaring up your little hilly knoll and refusing to leave. "We're staying here forever!" Joss incense, tie dyes, a few tiny cymbals and, yes, Illinois Valley, Oregon, cabernet sauvignon served with quesadillas. Suzi David, Queen Goddess of it all in her Tex-Mex attire, tended the vineyards, the quesadillas and the wine. While both were good, the entertainment was truly remarkable.

Through it all, this nagging problem invaded my thoughts: both wineries had too many different types of wines, each from divergent climates and temperaments. I returned to Portland with far more questions than answers.

Our assistant winemaker and I worked several events together. Hosting an event for visiting French business people, I called each winery and purchased a case of their best wine to pour. We produced some very good reserve pinot noir ourselves, and took pride in knowing the grape. We opened the one we had never seen before from Eyrie: a South Block Pinot Noir, 1975, and proceeded to taste. It was cherries and velvet, and as Burgundian as could be imagined.

We picked ourselves off the floor, as did the 50 French business people. A month later, the Eyrie South Block Pinot Noir 1975 was entered in a tasting of 300 of the world's best wines sponsored by Gault Millau travel and restaurant guide. It finished in the top 10. A re-tasting was held and the Eyrie pinot finished at No. 2.

Oregon had found her grape and the state was finally on the map. The fascinating thing about little-known, emerging wine regions is that it takes only one major event to tip the balance toward a grape or style. We have to admire the Europeans for their perseverance in discovering their wine identity. Most of all, we admire the person who first decides that the filbert orchard has to go, and replaces it with an unknown grape in an unproven location.

Oak Knoll's pinot noir took best in state at a show two years later.

Big Sky Country

Montana weighs in at 147,047 square miles, with its few cities separated by great distances. My new home town of Missoula was 40,000 or so souls. Part University town and part Wild West, it was perfectly normal in Missoula to see a University of Montana professor in head-to-toe tweeds walking down Higgins Avenue, and just behind him a cowboy in full chaps with six shooters low slung on his hips. No one even blinked.

Montana's moment in wine came in 1980 when the state legislature changed the law from an exclusive state store system of selling wine to one of free enterprise. This opened up a new world of wines for distributors, stores and restaurants, none of whom had any experience in the wine biz.

I wound up as sales manager for a distributor, wearing both my tweed jacket and my six shooters. Two wine producers, Gallo and Heublein, controlled 60 percent of the wine sold in America and they had mapped out Montana as their collision-course battleground. With the explosive gains in table wine sales that began in the late 1960s, there was a lot to win and lose. But most importantly, this was one of those rare opportunities: this was an entirely new wine state the two giants could use as a training ground for the upcoming decades' surge in wine consumption.

Grocery store shelves are the primordial battleground for brands in America. Take for example Campbell's Soup. In one 5-foot length of shelf, Campbell's has complete reign from top to bottom. To ensure that the fiefdom remains intact, the soup manufacturer has even created sub-brands like Chunky, Simply Home, Select, Hearty Choice, Kitchen Classics and

Family Size. These comprise the moat that protects the American soup fortress. The wine companies envy and emulate Campbell's for its unrivaled ability to capture and keep the competitor's space.

The Gallo-Heublein war lasted a little over a year, but it was the stuff of tall tales and urban legend. One of the most notorious showdowns took place in a large supermarket in the city of Bozeman. The Gallo rep and the Heublein rep had been wrestling for all-important shelf space for hours, with neither budging one wine-bottle slot. The wine aisle of the store was strewn with wine boxes and papers. One of the two threw a cigarette on the floor, where it landed and caught a piece of paper ablaze. Neither rep moved.

Just then, the store manager rounded the corner and began to scream "My store is on fire!" The manager had the two recalcitrant boys stomp out the fire, clean up the resulting mess, and be banished to the parking lot for life.

Things in general were not going so well. Gallo had generally squashed Heublein like a gnat on those shelves, and I was a Heublein distributor. We had all the brands, and they had all the space. I knew how it felt to be a Campbell's soup competitor.

When my less-than-brilliant distributor arch rival took Mr. Particularly Mean Store Manager golfing in a cart loaded with two cases of cold beer, the two proceeded to get ripped, wreck the cart, and get thrown off the course. My idiot competitor was rewarded with more shelf space because it was a "cool" outing. Things were definitely not going so well.

One of our best sellers was the hot imported wine of the decade: Lambrusco, a sweet, fizzy Italian red. We had Riunite, our competitor, Mr. Golf Cart Boy, had Cella. Everywhere in the universe Riunite outsold Cella 10-to-one, except, you guessed it: Missoula, Montana. The town was frequently visited by Cella Winery spoksman Mr. Aldo Cella. A pseudo-Italian who favored white suits, a white fedora, and whose tastes ran to the flamboyant, Mr. Cella appeared on television ads surrounded by a bevy of young Italian women crooning, "Aldo, Aldo." The truth of the matter was that he was a Greek-American actor with a penchant for vodka. The low point came when he was made Grand Marshall of the Montana state fair.

At the same time, we were graced by visits from Carl, our Riunite rep. A neurotic, nepotistic young wine-pro wannabe, Carl reminded me of Pee Wee Herman in training. He was always wired and ready to jump through the roof. Was it dad's gaze over his should or Aldo Cella's? Who knew.

Carl called and asked me to meet him at one of the grocery stores. As luck would have it, Carl chose Mr. Particularly Mean Manager's store. Carl grabbed a cart and proceeded to wheel it over to the wine section, muttering, "We'll take care of those Cella bastards once and for all." He stuck his little hands out of his Pee Wee suit and began grabbing bottles of Cella off the shelf, putting them in his cart as fast as he could. Carl had no doubt that this move would make them simply go away —perhaps to the dumpster.

By this point, I'm panicking; envisioning Mr. Particularly Mean Store Manager storming down the aisle and putting us both in the dumpster. I yanked Carl by his tiny collar, nepotism or not, and led him out into the parking lot and into his car. I gently and quietly put all the bottles back on the shelf. Carl was never heard from again. Rumor was he pulled a gun on his Bozeman distributor. But that was only rumor.

The all important Heublein national sales meeting was coming up soon, and it was time to sharpen up a few pointed questions. Heublein got its start with A-1 Steak Sauce, moving on to develop Smirnoff Vodka, and eventually buying its way into the wine biz by purchasing a handful of well-known national brands.

In preparing for the Heublein meeting, I had unearthed a glitch in Gallo's game plan: Gallo was filling store shelves with brands that didn't result in a good economic return for retailers. By disrupting Gallo's Campbell's-like fortress, our much-maligned brands would wind up with better shelf positions and higher sales, thus making the stores more money. Come the big day, I stood up in the meeting and asked the president of Heublein how we should rearrange these brands on the shelf. He looked at me like I was speaking Swahili, and turned to his national sales manager, who simply shrugged his shoulders. I knew at that moment that I was on my own.

When I returned to Missoula, I was informed that we would be given the honor of test marketing a new Heublein brand. T.J.Socials were 6-oz. throw-away plastic cups packaged with a small bottle of strange stuff. The substance was wine —multicolored at that —but was made to resemble liquor. I was never quite sure whether they were to take the liquor drinker to wine or the wine drinker to liquor. But we got their fanciful little display bins in all the stores nonetheless.

They sold like crazy for a while, until they started to change color. In the meantime, I had arranged a visit from our statewide Heublein rep. A day before his arrival, a huge cloud was forming in the Western sky. The rep called to make sure it was still OK to come, and I assured him it would be fine.

When he arrived the next morning Missoula looked like the landscape of the moon. That cloud was ash from the eruption of Mt. St. Helen's volcano, which was at least 400 miles away. We spent the day slowly traveling through the chalk-like dust that engulfed the town, a dust that provided a great backdrop for the eerie phosphorescent glow coming from each of our T.J. Socials bottles as they shined from their displays through the windows of closed stores. The rep made sure we never saw that product again.

The problem of Gallo having its boots solidly planted in my face wouldn't go away. I did, however, get along particularly well with one store manager for a large drug chain. He was a genius in that he sent his own cleaning crews into the dorms at the end of the semester, calculating all the stuff the students would need for the next classes. He was the kind of person who would try something new, and his store sold a large amount of wine.

My plan was to draw up the new shelf arrangement and present it to him on the weekend. He had four televisions in his office, one for each football game. This Sunday there were only two on. That meant that I had 20 minutes for a presentation before third quarter started on both TVs.

The plan worked, was a done deal, and was scheduled to take place the next week. Just before we went in to reset the shelves, a restaurant manager friend laughed and told me, "I found something for you when I was cleaning one of the bathrooms."

Oh, sure.

He had found a men's magazine with a hysterical cartoon. The sales and early reputation of the Ernest & Julio Gallo winery was built on skid row wines, though the company had upped the quality considerably by the time its products arrived in Montana. The cartoon was of three winos sprawled in an alley drinking cheap white port. One looks up and exclaims, "Not THE Ernest and Julio." This was too good to pass up. We had them made into color T-shirts.

We showed up three hours early for the moat-and-fortress shelf adjustment, and by the time Golf Cart Boy arrived with his winery cohorts to assess the damage, we were walking out the door wearing those most peculiar T-shirts. Their market was never the same. I could finally breathe easy when going into a store.

Now that the stores were no longer a nagging pain, it was time to look for interesting wines for the market. Montana was full of expatriate Californians who moved to Oregon and found it too crowded. They had money and they wanted interesting wine.

A few winery reps whose reputations preceded them came into the market. Such was the case with John Fraunfelder, a senior manager for Seagram Chateau and Estates Wines. In Oregon, people spoke of him in hushed tones reserved for describing saints. Unfortunately, I never ran into him while in Oregon.

When I finally did, I was surprised. For a person touted as being a guru of European wines, he did not cut an impressive figure. He looked older than his 50 years, was balding, slightly stooped and wore a suit that looked like he had just slept in it .The collars of his shirts were frayed, and his ties were at least a decade out of date. But when you sat near him while tasting a wine, he had the bearing of a four-star general in the field assessing the troops. Fraunfelder was the guru's guru. He single-handedly covered six Western states, and when he appeared, his distributors acted as though a member of royalty was coming to town. In the minefield that was European wine, with all its crooks and snakes, John became our beacon for authentic wines —frayed cuffs and all.

Montana is a place where untold amounts of beef are consumed. It's a cultural thing, and stems in part from the state's cold winters. Fraunfelder was a pioneer in matching wines to foods in specific regions. His idea in this case was to combine the luscious red wines of the Burgundy region of France with the lighter, softer flavors of prime rib. He nailed the type of flavors Montana drinkers sought, just as he had when he worked his magic introducing Alsatian pinot gris and salmon in Oregon.

We were turned onto to the likes of D'Angerville's Volnay, winemakers in the same village for 190 years. Theirs are wines of coolness and complexity. Tollot Beaut wines were the Burgundian equivalent of Montana itself, honest, hardworking and frugal but giving a lot for its work. Our favorite eccentric wine —from the Frank Nervo of France —was the Marcilly Brothers Reserve. The two old bachelors, living in an antique winery, delivered unusual chocolate notes and spices that seldom show up as flavors in pinot noir. It was no doubt due to those antique barrels.

Even local restaurants began offering exciting wines and wine-food pairings. A big Texan named Earl owned the company and ran the show. He wore a different pair of cowboy boots each day, each made from a different one of God's little creatures. My sales crew went by the name of the Bop a Dips, which was actually their stage name when they got together with Miss Kitty Litter to dress up and get down to playing some rock-and-roll.

The Bop a Dips insisted I head south to the tiny town of Hamilton to do a seminar on the glories of French white burgundy. I thought they were trying to get me bumped off by the crazed locals. At any rate, we grabbed a couple of cases of different Macon's and Pouilly Fuisse, and I found my too-tweedy little ass in an honest-to-god Wyatt Earp shootout saloon in Hamilton, Montana, talking to a group of men with extremely dark sweat stains on their cowboy hats. They reached for large wads of bills in their dusters. They were actually thrilled over the wines.

Turns out these were simply good ol' pot-growing boys from California who were using the accommodations of the Wild West to hang out. There were little hidden pockets of Californian expatriates everywhere. I brought in some Corton Charlemagne from Fraunfelder and it immediately sold out, much to my complete dismay. This is the vineyard planted by the man himself, Charlemagne, Emperor of the Franks in 800 A.D., and it has been stupidly expensive ever since. Someone out there was really enjoying this wine.

I met the Mystery Couple and they invited me to take a look at their digs. The first thing they warned me to do was not to take the wrong turn off their excruciatingly long dirt road. Otherwise, the leader of the neighborhood militia group would greet you with unbelievable armament.

Approaching their all-world log mansion, I noticed the view of the valley below was limitless with forest. The couple had done the California-Oregon-Montana junket, and now he was retired and owned the entire mountain and valley. Charlemagne would have been proud.

As time went on, reps flooded the market in The Invasion of the 1980's. Their main goal was to get a toehold. One young nepotist, who came in from Seattle, was clearly here to be trained between his jaunts back and forth to see his girlfriend. Both dad and granddad were famous wine brokers on the coast. I told the young man that the best thing he could do for us would be to bring some wine back from dad's cellar.

Clearly an excellent idea. Weeks later, the young nepotist returned in his pickup truck with several cases of wine from dad's stash. If he thought he made an impression, he was correct. It was a collection of rare Robert

Mondavi Cabernet Sauvignon from 1966 to 1978, with a few early Charles Krug Reserves thrown in for good measure. Dad approved; he just hoped they would go to some good. Don't worry dad, they did. I phoned up my restaurant buds and we put together a wonderful tasting. That young nepotist was all right, and those restaurants still carry Mondavi cabernets.

Gene Ford, our Christian Brothers winery rep and guru, resembled E. Frank Henriques in a suit. He too was a Roman Retread and enjoyed using our market as his winery's experimental station. The winery unfortunately had one foot in the past and half a foot in the present. By the mid 1980s, Christian Brothers had become a quirky anachronism by not vintage-dating its wines and by insisting on promoting grapes and wines whose popularity was tenuous at best.

Ford's piece de resistance, and the reason I thoroughly enjoyed seeing him, was the fact that he was an idea man. He devised a labeling system for California Chablis that showed sweetness levels with color bars, and he designed generic burgundy labels to show the softness of flavor.

Ford was also always tinkering and writing books to educate the layman. Today an illustrated guide, then a 10-minute wine course and a proposed work on wine and health. Unfortunately, no physician had ever signed off on alcohol as being good for you, but he kept plugging.

One of the quirkier customs in Montana is that of ordering a drink to go. Our favorite restaurant d'Aurias was located half an hour south of Missoula. After a nice dinner, one local banker usually bought all of his friends (and he had a lot of friends) a glass of wine to go. It was always poured into a large purple plastic cup.

I preferred to drink mine there, and always liked to check out the bottle —an occupational hazard. This time it was a little Clos de Tart, an $80 bottle of Grand Cru Burgundy. The banker, unfortunately, was arrested for embezzling funds. Served him right for serving a Grand Cru Burgundy in a plastic cup. Montana was all it lived up to be.

On My Own in France

By 1983, the dollar had crushed European currency, making imported wines unbelievably affordable. With a small loan from friends —and some luck —I could find some trustworthy French wine producers, act as an independent wine broker, and export wines to distributors I knew in the United States. The only hitch was that everything had to go well. To make any money, I had to ship 1,200 12-bottle cases at a shot.

After deciding to take the plunge, I found myself in an airport in Paris with nothing but a small suitcase full of clothes and a large one full of wine books. I had just picked up my bags when a Frenchman from the flight asked, "What do you do?"

As soon as I uttered the magic words "wine business," he hailed a cab and joined me for the ride to my accommodations, a small hotel in Paris recommended by a friend. The Frenchman boldly announced, "I am the president of a Bordeaux wine company." This came as a bit of a shock given the way he looked. Dressed in leather pants, a leather shirt and a bulky leather jacket, his slicked-back black hair fell to his shoulders. This was obviously the character John Travolta emulated for his role in Pulp Fiction. The Bordeaux wine company president promptly hopped in the cab and immediately fired up a joint of the "finest Aleppo hash." I was here to buy wine, and couldn't work with my brain flying out of my skull, so I passed on the hash.

As we went on a seemingly endless joyride around Paris, this character began his pitch on the glories of his Bordeaux properties. I had trouble hearing him, with my head stuck out the window and the bored cab driver yelling that we had passed my stop. The Travolta in France named Alain was all the while countering to the cab driver that we talking "Hea-vy biz-nes." One thing I picked up during these first few moments in Europe was that this guy, in spite of his quirks, knew the U.S. wine consumption market. Turned out we were both going to the same conference, so this was unfortunately not my last meeting with Alain.

Mercifully, the cab finally dropped me off at my hotel on the Rue Madelaine, with my head spinning but none the less for wear. My room wouldn't be ready for an hour, but I noticed a little bar next door where I could have a drink, relax and recover more from the cab ride than the flight. The bar was a cute, dimly lit place that served my purpose of sipping on a glass of Champagne and clearing the cobwebs from my head. The peace was suddenly broken when the two bathroom doors burst open and out stormed a dozen wildly dressed, crazed French prostitutes, each demanding a glass of Champagne from the dazed, "cute American." Between the Travolta wannabe, my throbbing head, and the hookers, I wasn't feeling quite so cute. Welcome to Paris.

The conference was held in the Southern French town of Cannes in an old hotel overlooking the beach. The big local buzz was that the diminutive rock star Prince was filming a movie there and couldn't get his tiny feet to reach the pedals of his Ferrari. A man could have worse problems.

Arriving at the conference were wine producers from all over Europe and a slew of American wine buyers. Many of the Europeans regarded Americans as one big walking Latvia Syndrome. They assumed we drank nothing but worthless, caffeine-tinged, sugared, carbonated soft drinks unfit for human consumption. Well, at least I knew where we stood.

What these Europeans failed to understand was that my generation was different from the one their parents knew. We knew European wines and vineyard practices, and were well aware of European wine-making strengths and weaknesses. What I didn't realize was that I didn't need that suitcase of books I brought along —I had already tasted and experienced their entire contents.

The conference consisted of a series of one-hour meetings, each with a different wine producer who had 8 to 10 wines per day. I tasted at least 100 wines a day, from everywhere. My first meeting was, of course, with Alain. He showed up in a completely different pair of leather pants, leather shirt and a bulky, expensive jacket. I would hate to handle this guy's luggage.

Apparently, Bordeaux had recovered admirably from the little problem created a decade earlier by the scandals of Mr. Pierre Bert. The region's wines were good, copious and inexpensive. But, more importantly, I discovered during our one-hour meeting that to be a good broker one had to forge bonds, relationships that transcended doing "Hea-vy Biz-nes." In other words, you have to have someone there you can really trust. After checking around, I discovered that Alain was a nepotist. Dad had set him up in New York in the business. His wines weren't bad, they just weren't exciting. If only he could have put some of that multi-layered coolness inside the bottles. Besides, his real claim to fame was being a chick magnet for the young, middle-aged and old. Must have been all that leather.

My next meeting was with Joseph Hallareau and Son, a long line of father-to-son grape farmers from Loire Valley. The second I walked into that room, I could sense their incredible uneasiness over dealing with an American. I was about to battle my worst case yet of convincing them we could overcome the Latvia Syndrome.

In this instance, I felt forced to do only one thing. I blurted out, "Just bring out a glass of wine, set it on the table and I will tell you the grape variety and where it is from." The blind tasting showdown is done only in the most extreme circumstances. Glasses were dutifully assembled, and I nailed their wines within a few miles of the actual vineyards.

Joseph Hallereau Sr., a large, roughhewn farmer who minced no words, was amazed that a lowly American could possess such tasting prowess. I proceeded to open my schedule and read off the days and hours I spent in the business every week. His stubby, partially smoked Gallious cigarette nearly fell out of his mouth, such was his amazement. The old man went into the other room and fumbled about in his luggage. He had a gift for such a diligent American wine taster. His winery produced a chart that recommended which wine cured which ailment and how many glasses would enact that cure. I still have his valuable —and thoroughly French — chart.

Maladity	Wine	Glass
Allergies	Medoc	1 glass
Constipation	Vouvray	4 glasses
Fever	Champagne	4 flutes
Gout	Sancerre	4 glasses
Hypertension	Alsatian	4 glasses
Obesity	Burgundy	4 glasses

After the rounds of meetings, the conference goers assembled in a creaky dining room for dinner. Each producer hauled out his finest wine for all to taste. The other Americans laughed when I brought out a few of my own I had managed to stash in my suitcase. They were none other than those old Amador County Zinfandels Rev E. Frank Henriques turned me on to.

The French were blown away. They always immediately check a wine's label for the alcohol content as theirs can be a too low to balance their wines. At a roaring 16 percent alcohol (this is an Amador Zinfandel after all), the wine caused a commotion. All the French growers tasted and commented profusely .They were amazed, confused, and generally agreed that this wine closely resembled the wines their fathers and grandfathers had made. At least they never referred to me as a cola-drinking Latvian again.

No matter how diligent you were in tasting wines at this conference, there was always some distraction. Cannes was cosmopolitan and a touch seedy. The absolute toughest distraction of all was that the rooms in the large hotel hosting the conference all meet faced the beach. While tasting a magnificent Chablis Grand Cru from a microscopic vineyard, I looked up to describe the wine to my host just in time to see a bevy of young, topless women a few yards from our window. I put my forehead on the table and said, "I just can't taste any more wine today."

After meeting and tasting wines from more than 50 producers, I finally encountered two gurus. Peter, the Brit, educated at the great wine school of Montpelier, France, and Glenn, the Brit from India, educated at the London School of Economics. They were doing the same thing I was: running a business by the seats of their pants and chasing producers all over France in search of fascinating wines.

The three of us tasted their latest finds along with the most current barrel samples from Bordeaux. The drink-them-now and slurp-them-down 1980 vintage, which was perfect for restaurants in the states; the classic

1981s, a collector's wine of high quality; and the recently tasted yet highly touted 1982s, which we found out of character, but great beyond belief.

I bought a lot of their Bordeaux, and we spent our free time talking about what was happening in each of the world's wine regions. They insisted that the real excitement was coming from Cannes' neighboring area of Montpellier in Languedoc. This vast area comprises the majority of southern France, and has been the heartland for bulk wine production for centuries. All told, 500 million gallons yearly —which was about one-third of France's total production —came from Languedoc. Languedoc was the world's largest forgotten wine region. It was unpredictable, and sometimes undrinkable, but it was always abundant.

We began by poring through recent French government regulation changes. France had mercifully created an entirely new category of wine with Languedoc in mind called Vin de Pays, or French country wine. For the first time, this new set of regulations would allow winemakers to put the names of the grape varieties on their labels. In turn, concentrating on producing quality grapes would create the impetus for growers to make interesting and exportable wines instead of unidentifiable plunk. It was worth a look.

Our next challenge was to travel through the region. One of the main differences in pursuing wine mania lifestyle in Europe was the type of car available for the journey. I rented a bizarre French car that resembled an armadillo on tiny wheels. Sitting in the driver's seat was like being crammed into a space capsule. Surprisingly, these tiny cars hold just as much stuff. The coffee in cups is stronger, the clothes and papers are squeezed into smaller seats, but the sample bottles are still everywhere. You drove on those narrow roads like a bat out of hell, but you got there nonetheless.

We began our hunt in the d'Aude, a large area that produced 150 million bottles annually, and was known for quality reds. We tasted and purchased wines from Corbieres, Minervois, and Fitou; all local, robust and earthy. Though we saw mostly old barrels, shiny stainless steel equipment was beginning to make inroads here. For us, the best wines were still as honest and forthright, a flavorful reflection of their unique place of origin.

After spending far too many mornings shivering in bone-chilling cold cellars, clutching my coffee cup just to keep my hands from freezing, we finally found enough producers to put together our own label, Juliette. We were among the first ever to export these wines under the new Vin de Pays regulation, bringing into the States a merlot, cabernet sauvignon, chardonnay, french colombard and a sauvignon blanc.

The work involved in putting our label together was not the typical wine maniac's tourist route. The closest we came to seeing a romantic vista was the medieval citadel of Carcassonne at dusk, all aglow and unbelievably imposing. This kind of wine traveling was the equivalent of riding in the team bus, and an old one at that.

The excitement, however, made the bumpy ride worth the trouble. The wines I sent to Oregon, Washington and California were hits: Burgundies, Bordeaux, Loire Valley and the Southern French varietals. After a couple of years, I noticed that Americans did not know the French varietals as a type of wine, in spite of drinking them and liking them. They still lacked an identity, which was the original problem with Languedoc.

After several years of importing wines and taking buying trips, the Languedoc identity problem became the least of my worries. The dollar was falling like a stone, and all of my brands would double in price if it continued. Years back, I had set a magic number onto a spreadsheet, telling myself that when I reached that, I would sell the rights to import my brands to a distributor and head off to another glorious career in wine mania. I went ahead and made the last trip, which was bittersweet. Frankly, I even missed Alain and his wild cab rides.

While I sold more Bordeaux, my last buying trip was to Burgundy. In Bordeaux, the people were cold and the food dull. Burgundy was lively, filled with unpredictable wines and people. When scouting for local wines, find the local wine guru. John Fraunfelder turned me on to this one: Armand Cottin, President of Laboure-Roi, a Burgundy firm in the tiny hamlet of Nuits St Georges.

Cottin's motto was, "Better to be the king in Nuits St. Georges, than a peasant in a large city." He found and bottled exciting wines from his own region and surrounding villages. Cottin was not merely a source for excellent wines and reliable information, but he also bridged the gap between the American and French consciousnesses. Tall, urbane, sophisticated, well-attired even in a sweater and slacks, and very well spoken, he cut right through our cultural differences.

As a teen during World War II, while his father was away fighting for the resistance, his mother and her family saved and hid downed American fliers from the German patrols. After the war, when an American came to visit, the family hauled out Old Glory and flew it proudly in front of the house. In between sips of his delicious Nuits St. Georges, Cottin reminisced, telling us in his soothing voice that he looked forward to the 50th anniversary when all the aviators would return for a reunion with his family.

Cottin put together a typically great farewell French lunch that lasted three hours and included much wine and toasting to both our great countries. We concluded with a tour of one of the great shrines of French wine: the magnificent Clos de Vougeot. Once a Cistercian monastery in the 12th century, it was now a museum/gift shop with a 125-acre vineyard of sloping Burgundy greatness.

Unfortunately, all I could think of was my bladder, filled with glasses of wine. Armand, knight that he was, explained the local customs. Passing armies always saluted the great vineyard of Clos de Vougeot. He, on the other hand, considered the duty of relieving oneself on the great vineyard a sign of respect.

There was one last visit to make before leaving Burgundy. One reward for going out and doing your share of "Mission Impossible" brand-building is the little favors you collect along the way. Now was the time to cash in on a big one: a tour of the famous and increasingly impossible to see Domaine de la Romanee Conti. This minuscule vineyard gained celebrity status when the Louis XIV's physician recommended that The Sun King switch from Champagne to Burgundy to cure his gout. And I thought the Hallareau boys with their chart were just kidding. I guess the switch worked, because the king and every other noble in France wanted the producer's roughly 8,000 bottles a year.

Today, every billionaire and royal wannabe would gladly kill to own a few bottles at whatever the price. The vineyard, a mere 4.46 acres, is atop a hill surrounded by some of the world's greatest sites for pinot noir, but Romanee Conti itself reigns supreme as the place where elevation, sun and nutrients all come together to create the stuff of legend. The winery consists of little more than a small courtyard where we found two older local women directing the movement of potted plants to a man on a small forklift. He hopped down, introduced himself as Herve the winemaker, grabbed a couple of glasses and a long glass tube known as a wine thief, and off we went to the cellars.

Most surprising was the lack of wine-making equipment, the most prominent object being a tray for sorting fruit. They aged the wine very simply in all new oak, made by their own coopers every year from three-year-old, air-dried wood given a light toast. We tasted through wines from their entire range of vineyards.

A small man, Herve was careful and precise in both his movements and thoughts. These were difficult years, 1983 and 1984. The importers wanted the wines now, but the critics wanted them to age and soften up a bit. Making wine in this place had to be one of the highest-pressure jobs in all of wine mania.

The look I carried, standing in front of those lone 13 barrels of Romanee Conti, tasting (make that drinking) this spicy, earthy, opulent, exotic wine that just happened to be made from pinot noir, elicited from Herve the well chosen thought, "You guys from Oregon are really into this." Yes, Herve, we are maniacs, and it is rumored that this wine will even cure your gout.

Once back in the States, I took time to reflect on my adventures in finding and creating brands, as did many who were on the importing side of the wine mania in the 1980s. Ironically, Vin de Pays wines finally did catch fire, but not until around 2000, when the completely improbable brand Fat Bastard created a stir.

Every time I look at a bottle of that wine now, I chuckle. Not just because the fat hippo on the label is humorous, but because people drinking the wine *still* don't know what it is or where it comes from. So much for the best-laid plans of French bureaucrats and maniac wine brokers, and so much for curing our beloved Latvia Syndrome.

Virginia Wines: Form versus Substance

It was unlike any other job interview. The President of Montdomaine Cellars was sitting opposite me in the lobby of a very swank hotel in San Francisco. His only request was for me to arrange a table for lunch for us in the best restaurant in San Francisco with half an hour's notice.

I pulled out my emergency business card from Jim, a friend from Oregon who was president of the American concierges' professional group. This was like waving a sacred talisman in front of the concierge. We had the best table in the city's finest restaurant in 15 minutes.

Over lunch, the winery president related his story about his three partners planting vineyards in Virginia on sites Thomas Jefferson predicted would be the first great American wine region. A simple winery had been built there in 1981 and stocked with the latest equipment. My task would be to both run the winery and elevate it to the status of finest winery in the East. He and his partners were investing in making Thomas Jefferson' dream a reality. Now *that* was pretty straightforward.

Charlottesville, Virginia, was a small town of about 40,000 people, but it had a New York attitude. Mr. Jefferson had originated, designed, built and written the curriculum for the Charlottesville's crown jewel the University of Virginia. You could barely walk down the street without bumping into at least two Nobel Laureates. It was impossible to attend a party without Mr. Jefferson's name being mentioned as though he were standing in the room. It was this fixation on history that lent the town its aura.

Heading off for my usual neighborhood winery tours seemed strange here. There was no maniac wine mentality like in Oregon. Everyone here seemed to be living a genteel country lifestyle, making indifferent wines to sell to tourists. Form versus substance clearly ruled the day.

Montdomaine was different. First of all, it resembled a trailer park set inside a rock quarry next to a concrete bunker. There was a complete lack of form, but lots of substance. In spite of the fact that the wines were solid in both quality and price, few accounts would buy or promote them. When I went to visit my local distributor Jabba the Bubba, he had his requisite Bubba Barbeque slathered all over an already hideously cluttered desk. His homily was delivered in a deep Southern growl: "Don't worry, it will happen soon. The wines aren't ready yet, the people aren't ready yet."

I quickly discovered that this operation lacked a certain drive and ambition. I also discovered that everything here was not as it seemed. Jabba the Bubba was a nepotist, and all his Junior Jabbas were in the finest private schools. The family owned a piece of Jefferson's original land that the fine folks at Monticello would have killed for.

But Jabba made several key mistakes. The first was buying a Porsche for his daughter. The second, and by far the worst, was taking it back and giving it to his mistress. Mrs. Jabba wound up with both the business and the land. My main contact was Jabba's top sales rep Bob-O, a loyal good ol' boy who covered a sales territory just slightly smaller than Western Siberia.

Mrs. Bob-O had gotten fed up with the large number of family pets and had banished one to Mr. Bob-O's car. I've had a car full of papers, samples and laundry, but never the addition of a hyper Chihuahua climbing all over the place. The tiny creature was great at eliciting sympathy from buyers who gazed out the window into its tearful eyes as it peered over the steering wheel after his master.

After a few hundred calls promoting my newfound family and great success selling Montdomaine, I decided it was time to check out the competition. That's when I met Felicia. Felicia was the Dowager Empress of Virginia wine. It was coming together now: the countrified lifestyle, form versus substance … she was their Marie Antoinette with her tiny picture-perfect estate, the lake entrance, the geese, the Polled Hereford farm that was miscast as a vineyard, and her middling quality wine. The key ingredient here was the classic combo of politics and power. In her 60s, Felicia personified New York goes to the country. The perfect coif, the understated gold accessories, and above all, the ability to snap her fingers at a party and have high-ranking state officials pad over like school boys.

Felicia personally founded and chaired (President for Life was the term du jour) every local wine society and organization. She was an amateur, knowing nothing about wine, and a nepotist, coming from money and marrying it three times. Her most enduring quality was as a wine maniac. There wasn't an event that she didn't dominate. She was regarded as a guru by her local lords and ladies in waiting, but to grant her true guru status you would have to set the bar awfully low.

Felicia's crowning achievement occurred during President Reagan's visit to Russia to meet Gorbachev. No one would ever sing, but somehow, bottles of her innocuous white wine made it to Russia and were served to Reagan and Gorbachev. This occurrence was ballyhooed for what seemed like years, but it did nothing to elevate the status of or interest in Virginia wine. "Gorby Wine" was basically a non event.

Through it all, Montdomaine was actually doing better. The investors had done nothing to transform our little trailer park in the quarry, but the winery was winning awards and gaining recognition. I put yet another 200,000 miles on my car, conducting tent revival meetings on the glory of Virginia wine with distributors, stores and restaurateurs.

Virginia has a tough climate for growing grapes. Winters are too cold, spring is unpredictable, and harvest time far too humid. The soil is a thick, impenetrable red clay that made it all but impossible for the vine roots to go a respectable distance for nutrients; and the sunlight is just under what grapes need to fully ripen. The end result can either be a fine European-tasting red, or a wine that resembles the flavor and texture of aluminum foil.

Through it all, we managed to make respectable wines, and there were a small but growing number of quality wines emerging from the flock of mediocrity. Naked Mountain Chardonnay was fat and toasty. Prince Michel's Barrel Select Chardonnay was a wine to emulate. Autumn Hill's Riesling and the Rapidan River Riesling were both excellent. Among the handful of good reds was the Linden Vineyards Cabernet Sauvignon.

Selling the wines presented another set of frustrations. In the mid 1980's, there was next to no interest in local wines except what we could stir up through the obvious cash cow of tourism. But in this world of amateurs, there would spring the rare and occasional guru.

Such was Gabrielle Rausse, the Italian vineyard specialist brought over to plant the well-sighted land at Barboursville. Rausse was now running a winery named Colle, the second vineyard Thomas Jefferson planted after Monticello. Rausse was wiry and well-tanned after decades of vineyard work. He talked in a lilting, heavily accented English that was as much song as speech. Rausse offered to give me a tour of the region's vineyards in his ancient Chevy farm truck. I was astonished at how good some of the non-planted potential sites were and how lousy some of the existing sites were.

Rausse was there in 1979 when all the government agricultural agencies and the university extensions told him and his boss at Barboursville not to even think about planting European grapes because they wouldn't make it through the brutal winter, unpredictable spring and humid summer. We went back to the winery and the guru/pioneer opened some great wines that were not supposed to have happened. One of our growers in passing once said, "Some day there will be a statue of Gabrielle in Charlottesville." I heartily agreed. It was nice to have a moment of optimism, but in Virginia wine it was still form versus substance.

The classic amateur on the scene came in the form of local food and wine writer Hilde Lee. Lee's new book Virginia Wine Country contained the usual mishmash of winery recipes for the housewife, as well as some of the most delusional thoughts ever delivered on the subject of local wine. "At $6-8, a bottle of Virginia chardonnay is certainly a better buy than a $12-15 bottle of overpriced California chardonnay." Having consumed more than my fair share of both region's chardonnay, I argued that you would have to be born lacking both a brain and tastebuds to make that asinine statement. Virginia wines were getting better, but they were in no way remotely close to having their own Paris tasting and crushing California.

But, wait, it gets better. The piece de resistance of the book was her analysis of why few restaurants chose to feature the local wines. "A restaurant that relies on a California wine consultant to develop its wine list is likely not to have a very wide or good selection of Virginia wines." To the best of my knowledge, no one ever air-dropped a flock of California wine consultants into Virginia wine country. The problem was simply that the local restaurateurs found local wines inferior in quality.

Contented little Charlottesville was in for a gigantic awakening in 1987. The place that always prided itself on coolness and aloofness was abuzz. John, Patricia, and tiny John Jr. Kluge moved into the neighborhood. John Kluge was America's wealthiest person. Just before the Kluges moved to Charlottesville, the latest edition of Town and Country Magazine ran a feature on the estate. Local stores piled them as high as the Sunday paper, and they sold out just as fast.

Town and Country taught us a variety of things about our new neighbors. They had purchased more than 6,000 acres in the "verdant, rolling farmland" of the area. They had built a 45-room mansion with adjoining chapel, barns, and hunting outbuildings. Our new neighbors had hobbies like playing on their own Arnold Palmer designed golf course, carriage riding (from their world-famous collection) and pheasant hunting from their own well-stocked preserve. It was all laid out in magnificent full color for us locals to gawk at. The Skazzi-designed gowns for Patricia as well as the priceless Waterford chandelier and George III silver. The locals were completely bowled over.

At the same time, crazy things were happening at the winery. The partners were experiencing pre-retirement amateur syndrome —in other words, they were feverishly casting about for someone else's money to use in finally building a decent winery. The county government was tiring of reviewing extensions to the trailer quarry.

On top of all of this, a little drama I call "The Revolt of the Growers" was set into motion. Bobby, leader of the revolt, was the most cantankerous of grape grows. An invitation from Bobby was tantamount to a call from one of the lesser deities. He was so high up in the Virginia genealogical hierarchy that he simply referred to the Kluges as people who will be here for awhile then gone —sort of like the Yankees.

Bobby was in his 60s, and hardened by a life taking care of his family's centuries-old plantation. He was tough, sun-baked and wore these pants, shirt and hat that resembled something made in the 19th century. You didn't want to mistake his soft patrician Southern drawl for weakness. His vineyards were as good as any could be in the Eastern United States. His forebears were friends and neighbors of the Jeffersons. He had the sites, the sun and the vines to put him in a commanding situation. He knew it and I knew it.

Unfortunately, he wanted me to persuade our little band of grower investors to put him back on the board of directors. He was supposedly banished for instigating a coup, but no one would talk. At a meeting at his house —which was a shrine of Jeffersonian artifacts collected over eons —I persuaded him to let us continue buying his grapes without adding to what was already a disintegrating situation.

The truth finally came out: he wanted a winery going up to honor Jefferson to be on his family's land, not our beloved little trailer park site. I erupted. At this point, a lesson in ancestor worship was what I didn't need. Hell, his grapes were vital to the quality of our wine, but there was no way the grower investors were going to let him take over the winery. We got nose to nose, and backed away.

He took me over to a small, framed brass object on the wall. He related that three of these were made for General Lafayette. One was given to President Washington, one to Benjamin Franklin and one to Thomas Jefferson. This was Jefferson's. They were medals of freedom made from the brass locks of the Bastille. I kept buying his grapes, but didn't have much to say to him again. Our goals and our worlds were very different.

The Kluges were settling in and buying more tracts of land, including one house Jefferson designed named Morven. Along with the house came a good established vineyard and 10 percent ownership of Montdomaine. The winery owners were delirious. They pictured John Kluge as a giant sack full of money circling overhead, ready to drop his bounty on them. When we all cozied up the Kluge retinue, we were floored to discover they were planning to build a museum to exhibit and house their stellar collection of antique carriages on the road facing the winery.

Then the bottom fell out. Some local guy's dog was missing. He bitched long enough to persuade a law-enforcement officer to look at Kluge's property, and that's when it all hit the fan. Kluge liked to import experts from Europe to handle his hobbies. Unfortunately the Scot in charge of Kluge's pheasants wasn't versed in the niceties of U.S. federal law regarding endangered species. He not only killed the hapless dog to prevent it from eating the pheasants, but he unfortunately shot down many of the red-tailed hawks in the vicinity.

The flap with the courts and the locals lasted a year with Kluge laying low on any further acquisition or development. That meant us. We hung tight in trailer land. Strangely enough, I did manage to get my own two Gorby events. I discovered a Presidential conference and dinner was to be held at Monticello. You can always trot out Thomas Jefferson as a symbol of everything. I knew Felicia would be breathing down the White House usher's neck to serve her wine to yet another head of state.

I caught up with the organizer, who was making his rounds assembling the millions of details an event like this requires. He tasted the wines, he liked the wines, and they would be served to all the governors and to the President. Wow. Montdomaine Chardonnay washed down a little Turban of Seafood Monticello with Aurora Sauce and Sesame-seed Galettes. Felicia did not take this well, being left out and all. We saw one another at one of her events shortly afterward. She didn't say anything to me, but the motion she made, running the dull side of her knife across her throat, was a priceless statement.

The second event came in the form of a road trip to the Wine Spectator, the world's most widely read consumer wine publication. My plan was simple: tell them the story of Jefferson's dream of planting vineyards near his home of Monticello, and how that dream had finally come true. The local wineries thought the trip was foolish and that the only way to get a story was to place an ad for $100,000. I wasn't so sure.

Sitting in their offices, I felt like Bob-O's dog with his tiny paws on the steering wheel of his master's car. The editor was cordial, but not overflowing with excitement when he heard my story. I handed him the wines and felt that if he tasted them at all it would be with indifference. The east coast just didn't have clout. He relented and said the freelance writer who covered the east coast would contact me. And he did.

The Wine Spectator article "Pursuing Jefferson's Dream in Virginia" broke on Feb. 28, 1989, as the first national story ever done on Virginia wine. They told the story well, but there was something missing. Great photos and quotes don't shake up the wine world, 90-point scores do. What I got was "Gorby Wine" all dressed up, and what I wanted was the Paris tasting.

There more things I could do to get the word out on Virginia wine, and one of them was to play the politics game. I decided that it was time to dip my toes in the water and made a bid for a marketing position in the industry.

My guiding guru for this adventure was the wildly eccentric Archie Smith III from Meredyth Virginia winery. Meredyth had bounced back and forth over the years, producing award-winning wines one moment and peculiar stuff the next. Archie must have been Keith Richard's twin separated at birth. He had classic '60s-style black, curly, disheveled and devilishly long hair jutting out in all directions; which he accessorized with a decades-old Levi's shirt and pants that hung from his frame like those on a scare crow. He spoke slowly and thoughtfully through the lungs of a lifetime smoker. I had heard that Archie came back from academia to run the family winery.

Our first industry political pairing was to address a conference of all Virginia wine distributors to encourage them to sell more Virginia wine. One of the participants asked that we recite our resumes to their group. My background caught them by surprise; they didn't expect years of expertise from someone in Virginia wine. Archie, clad in his usual attire, raised himself to the dais, looked at the room full of distributors and slowly recited "B.A. in Philosophy from the University of Virginia, M.A. in Philosophy and PhD in Philosophy from Oxford University. Reader in Philosophy, Oxford University." The room was deadly silent as he stared straight ahead and said, "My philosophy is that you sell my wine." The place went wild.

We were finally seeing some solid marketing of Virginia wine with more substance than form. My idea of creating a month expressly devoted to Virginia wine was accepted. October became Virginia Wine Month and the governor signed it. Archie and I were appointed by the governor to the Wine

Growers Advisory Board, becoming two of the 13 elders of the tribe who created the programs and allocated the money for research and marketing. The governor had just issued our marching orders to assemble and report back to him with all known facts about the Virginia wine industry. We separated into committees, and when our research was said and done, we would issue a report to the governor with recommendations.

After months of plowing and crunching every known number, the first ever report on The Status of the Virginia Wine Industry was complete. It was all there: the very good and the very bad. The dramatic turnaround, doubling sales figures over the past five years. The 100 percent increase in tourism in October. But lurking beneath the oh-so-cherry charts, graphs and news were some real zingers. Twenty-five percent of all vineyards were planted in the wrong sites for grapes and "would never be economically successful." Ouch. Maybe those Polled Hereford farms weren't such a good place for vineyards after all.

Two other findings were alarming, and unfortunately, no one was running with a bucket of water to put out the fire. Twenty-two of the 95 wines submitted to the Governor's Cup Wine Competition were flawed. But the absolute killer was that after polling the wineries, only two of 40 wanted a mandatory Quality Assurance Program that would test wines and award gold stickers for quality bottles. Hell, there were five wineries represented by actual board members. So much for vineyards, competitions and quality control; tourism still reigned supreme.

Ironically, while still mired in deepest Virginia wine politics and trying to digest the last bits of informational gristle from all our research, the Kluges not only made a re-appearance, but seemed interested in finally purchasing the winery. We received an invitation to Patricia's 40th birthday party at the Waldorf Astoria. This promised to be the major glitz-and-glitter event of the glitz-and-glitter decade. And since the Kluges' still owned 10 percent of Montdomaine, I couldn't get up to New York fast enough to sell some Montdomaine to the food and beverage guru at the Waldorf.

The hotel staff could talk about nothing but this event. Even by their standards, this event was extravagant. The entrance to the grand ballroom was framed by a castle of fresh flowers with caviar stations that were instantly laid bare. The Hollywood set, the New York set and the Charlottesvillians all eyed one another over a grand buffet. The interior space was covered entirely with fresh flowers. Drinking Montdomaine chardonnay amid the art deco while listening to a killer little rock-and-roll band was simply cool.

We then received the invitation to come to the Kluge estate and discuss the purchase of the winery. We brought our president, several board members and our accountant with his thick pile of documents. The timing was perfect because the board was in the process of gnawing one another to death, and the Kluge sale would end it once and for all. No more trailer land. Kluge brought himself, no papers, not even a calculator. He was a larger-than-life, grandfatherly business figure in an immaculately attired suit, with a gracious smile, quiet demeanor and a mind that operated with the force of a buzz saw. He quietly did the entire deal completely off the top of his head, much to the astonishment of our well-versed investor growers who were captains of the industry themselves.

That is how you become a billionaire.

As we were leaving, he gave us the grand tour of the house. We peered into his study, noticing a row of expensive shot guns, and he quipped,

"Those are my hawk hunting guns." Our jaws dropped. "Just kidding," he chuckled.

A few weeks later, as I was taking my Saturday stroll into town, the local paper caught my eye and I stopped dead in my tracks. The banner read, "Kluges Divorcing." That was it. The end, the deal is dead. No carriage museum, no purchase of the winery.

I was sitting in my office the following Monday, dazed and aimless when the phone rang. It was one of the top marketing people at the Virginia Dept. of Agriculture asking to see me. This was unusual because the wine industry rarely caused so much as a snicker at that level of the bureaucratic food chain. This guy was senior and retiring soon, and he had something to get off his chest.

We sat peering at one another across his very official desk. He went through his rant about the form-versus-substance issues in the Governor's Report, but I thought he could have done that over the phone. Something else was going on here.

He picked up a letter and shook it violently, his large frame, bushy eyebrows and thinning hair all moving at the same pace. He spoke like a tough old football coach in a tense locker room. The letter was from a Virginia winery requesting to bring in an unauthorized amount of out-of-state wine to sell under its label. His face turned beet red. "It is not the poorly planned vineyards or the lousy local wine that will sink your industry, but this. You will drown in an ocean of bulk out-of-state wine and people here will never know the difference." He signed and approved the request in disgust.

I left the office in a dazed state. Even as the chairman of the Wine Board, I was never privy to anything like this. I had just visited the darkest depths of Virginia wine. My head spun all the way back to Charlottesville, wondering what Dave Adelsheim would do, the toughest little crusader in Oregon against wineries getting big at any cost.

I dropped by a friend's store in Charlottesville and aimlessly stocked wines on the shelf for something to occupy my mind. While pulling a bottle from a case, it struck me: I was looking at the future. I held a blue bottle with striking graphics of a cartoon dog flying over the moon. But the most striking thing of all was the fact that the word "VIRGINIA" as the place of origin for grapes didn't appear on the label.

So that was what he was talking about. Wines trucked in from anywhere, masquerading as local. The wine, of course would be sweet, and wildly popular. It looked like there would be no Paris tasting where Virginia bested the world. Likewise there would be no Montdomaine either.

Years later, I found myself at a tasting admiring a regional winemaker's work. He asked where I had been involved in Virginia wines and I mentioned Montdomaine. His jaw dropped, his eyes narrowed, and he grasped both of my hands and said, "You were the pioneers. All of our quality standards are based on the work you guys did." There is nothing like being ahead of your time.

The Gigantic Wine Distributor

A gigantic wine distributor made me an offer to be their fine-wine specialist. One of the company's senior managers had just taken advantage of a momentary lapse in the state's distributor franchise laws to run off with a few corporate gems. The culprit was locally referred to as "Nick the Knife," for only a genuinely corrosive character would team up with an entrepreneur in garbage removal and proceed to remove both brands and staff from his former employer. Nick was swarthy, with thinning hair; a short, pointed graying beard; and a beak-like nose. He talked fast, and something about him made you periodically check your wallet.

My new employer, though missing some good brands and veteran people, was still gigantic and organized to military precision. Everyone wore a crisp white shirt, a suitably conservative tie and shined shoes; and drove identical Ford Tauruses devoid of coffee cups, papers, laundry and all the other things that I had come to love in my ride. I was certain I would feel transition pains —which I did for the entire time I worked there.

The gigantic distributorship was founded as a small company by The Jim, who then built it to its present size, and turned it over to his son Semi Jim. The rule of thumb for growing a small company to a gigantic company is work hard, drive your people like hell, and fuel it all on 40 cups of coffee per day per person. The Jim was the classic, up-by-your-bootstraps, tough-as-nails, old school wine distributor. He would get on his little golf cart at four o' clock every morning and tear through his massive warehouse, accompanied by his favorite shotgun and his favorite skid-row beverage, a bottle of Thunderbird. Just a little ride to check for any pilferage by the night crew. Since he periodically slept on the couch in his office, he could make this little run basically at any time of the day or night.

The Jim, who is now in his 70s, seldom addressed our seemingly millions of meetings, but when he did it was the stuff of legend. He would bark and snarl with his classic Chesty Puller, old Marine General physique. His favorite inspirational story was how he, as a young Marine on Iwo Jima, took his trusty pliers and "pulled the gold out of the dead Jap's teeth." I am not sure if this little story had a moral, but it certainly quieted the room down.

The usual problem with nepotism is that no matter how hard you try to pass your traits down the genetic ladder, some of them just don't travel well. While dad was flamboyant in his own peculiar way, the Semi Jim was a not very brilliant combination of nervous energy and paranoia. He was big and soft and pink. During our first foray to assess the damage wrought by Nick the Knife and his cohorts, the Semi Jim managed to drive his very large BMW, drink a cup of coffee with one hand, talk on the car phone with the other to one of his sales reps, ascertain that the rep was out of his assigned territory to pay a late furniture payment, and then fire said rep —all while crossing over a solid yellow line or two in the car. I came to love these little white-knuckled rides with the boss.

The life of someone who works for a gigantic wine distributor is filled with panic, some real, some imagined. The boss' phone number followed by 911 on my pager would produce such a moment. Naturally, it would be raining in torrents and, since I only had a pager, I got to cross several lanes of traffic to find the nearest phone booth at a fast-food place. As luck would have it, the Semi Jim was interviewing some schlemiel for yet another sales opening. Semi Jim asked the schlemiel one two many questions (read that as "two") and was out-foxed.

Now, I got to frantically drive back to the warehouse, haul the schlemiel into the conference room, and give him a Wine 101 once over. When I came in on these occasions, pissed off and soaking wet, having to bail out my nepotist boss, the schlemiel wouldn't have a prayer. But, chances are he would be hired anyway because the gigantic distributor always needed a warm body to throw on the streets. I got back in my car, drove back into the rain, and awaited the next 911 page.

There was a certain comic Chaplanesque air around guys like this, but make no mistake about the fact that there is also a deadly seriousness to their work and their survival. Distributors of this size, if they use their money and power, can dominate and control how wine is distributed.

One day, senior management was called into the large conference room for a meeting. We were there to discuss strategy for talking to legislators at the upcoming annual meeting of the state general assembly. Suddenly, in walked The Jim with the most powerful person in the general assembly: the speaker of the house. After a short speech was delivered to our eager little band, the speaker threw his arm around The Jim, looked him in the eyes and said, "When I am in the general assembly, you are in the general assembly." I termed it "The Best Democracy Money Can Buy Speech."

A large part of my job was looking after the distributor's fine wines. Before he departed, Nick the Knife had purchased some expensive wines in less-than-stellar vintages at the wrong prices; the types of wines I had scouted out in Europe. Their wines had been stored in the warmest part of the warehouse, leaving them in sorry shape if not already dead. I recommended we dump the stuff, but was outvoted by the two Jims. I loathe closeouts. They are mistakes recycled from winery to wholesaler to retailer to consumer.

So here I am, stuck with many cases of the crown jewels of Europe — Chateau Lafite, Latour and Petrus —in a very tarnished state. I struck a deal with a couple of retailers. I would sell them very, very cheap if they would throw them in a bin and sell them as "souvenirs," informing customers that these were more about labels than wine. That was certainly easy and reasonable.

Upon a return visit to one of the retailers, I found him chatting up a tourist in plaid shorts and a garish flowered shirt, his chest hair adorned by way too many gold trinket chains. They were talking in conspiratorial tones, when the retailer vanished into his secret Aladdin cave (his back room) and appeared with the "Magic wines." The prices were, of course, a little less than those of New York retail, but where else can you get such lovely wines that have been burnt to a crisp? Having been burnt myself, that was the last time I was involved with closeout wine. Get somebody else to do that dirty work. The distributor did end up putting in a temperature-controlled wine box, though it cut off a significant portion of the great golf-cart raceway.

The early 1990s was a period of declining economy paired with a rabid consumer interest in low-priced wines. Wineries and brokers were presenting bargain brands to us day and night. One broker, who I had known for years, insisted on meeting with the entire management team because his line was so exciting we "all needed to experience them." Being the official taster, I found his Vivache Chardonnay from Northern Italy lifeless. But, everyone has their secret hot button and this guy had won two silver stars as a marine in Vietnam, so The Jim was all over it. My next assignment was to go out and sell the 1,200 cases we had just purchased.

I hiked out to restaurants with our newfound treasure and actually did pretty well. It went with the local seafood and was innocuous enough not to bother anyone. In my daily forays through this large and complex market, I kept hearing about this one restaurant sales rep. He was something of a local legend among the beach habitués. Jim Stansberry, a maniac, sold wines during the same hours the all-night lifestyle restaurant managers and deranged chefs plied their trades. I was floored upon meeting him. He was slight of build, attired in basic Mardi Gras (without boa or beads), and he knew his wines. But Jim lived the coked-out life of his restaurant buddies. It was etched in the hundreds of scars on his face he got from sailing through the front window of his car. Jim was the poster boy for the excesses of the restaurant lifestyle. In all his battered glory, he was still a fierce competitor: the guru of the nocturnal.

Living out of your car and chasing the here-today, broke-tomorrow restaurant was a tough lifestyle, and an unenviable one in which to be single. I met many extremely attractive women, but they all seemed to have a combined IQ hovering around 78. Inter-company dating was forbidden, but the distributor never had an official written policy. You just got run over with the golf cart. People from the office and restaurant sales division began going out to local restaurants in groups of 8 to 10. The group faded down to 6, then 4, then 2. Judy, from the office, and I stared across the table at one another and that was it. We began practicing a form of dating we referred to as "hiding out."

We all went to occasional company events in peoples' houses, most notably potluck food-and-wine pairings done by the restaurant sales staff.

While I was working on my pasta dish over the stove, The Jim planted himself next to Judy (my secret misdemeanor date) and commenced to question my lengthy divorced status and bachelorhood and proclaimed that there was a direct link between pasta cooking expertise and effeminate matters. His classic comment was, "You know how those gay people like to cook." Judy was practically having an aneurysm. This was a delicious moment, being secretly in love with the beautiful woman beside you, cooking pasta and being called gay all at the same time. Pasta never tasted quite so good.

The hours at a gigantic distributorship were long, but one of your little bonuses came in the form of being given the opportunity to work with problem restaurant accounts. Le Chateau was the closest thing this area had to the fading star of cuisine: the continental restaurant. While most everything else in the area was casual dining or bistro style, this place at least pretended to be the real thing. Frank, owner and maitre'd, was a classic, old-school, whip-cracking maniac with his tall pouf of poodle-cut white hair in a pompadour and his out-of-style lounge suit —all the better to slide the dowagers' chairs to the table with as much fanfare as possible.

I wound up with him because no one else wanted him. This was trouble-shooting in wine mania at its finest. He actually had a pretty good wine list, representing a cross-section of quality wines that paired well with the food. Frank's attitude was very simple: "I don't give a shit about these wines." While masquerading as a mysterious French type, his classic behind the scenes line was, "I was a poor Polish boy who escaped from the stetel. Now, what do you have for free?" Legally, we had nothing for free. But, Frank knew how to figure an angle with the best of them. By law, all wine and beer had to be paid for at the time of delivery (those powerful distributors had powerful lobbyists), but the Perrier water was on 30-day terms. So he loaded up on Perrier and poured it freely at the tables. Of course, it showed up on your dinner bill later. He never paid for the Perrier. We finally hounded him, threatened him, and lost the entire account. He found another large distributor to play for a while.

Since our evening sales meetings were at least a break from Frank, I figured it couldn't get much worse. But his evening, The Jim took the podium. That was always menacing in itself. You just did your best to sit a safe distance and slouch down in your seat, avoiding all eye contact. Tonight we would listen to our special guest, Homer Somebody or Other. He was a serious old hay-seed from South Carolina that The Jim probably picked up as a hitch hiker.

The Jim started his introduction with, "Some of you out there may not believe this miracle beverage that Homer Somebody or Other has created. You doubters (and I swear he was looking right at me) need only try this great product as I have and you will believe in its cures." Whew! By this time I was practically crawling under my chair.

This miracle product was called Jogging in a Jug. It came in a half-gallon whisky bottle with a handle, and a simple line drawing of two joggers on the label. It was a vinegar and something else solution you drank twice a day to both cure and heal you at the same time. This was quickly turning into a real bite-the-head-off-the-snake show with Homer Somebody or Other droning on for hours about the miracle properties of his elixir. We were each issued our precious half-gallon jugs on the way out. I deposited mine in the trash can at the nearest Seven-11. The product did well in the drug stores for a couple of months and then fell off the planet. Homer Somebody or Other should have sold his company to The Jim that night.

The one meeting you knew to dread was the one where a winery sends five people in to have a serious little chat with all of you. Just take a few days off and avoid that one altogether. Kobrand, one of our largest fine-wine suppliers, had top-selling restaurant brands such as Louis Jadot from France, Cakebread from the Napa Valley, and Taittinger Champagne. They brought their heavy hitters to the conference room, including one fellow we had never met who was nicknamed "The Hammer." Oh, good, The Hammer meets The Jim.

The Kobrand force was there to roll out its new dynamic line of varietal wines from the South of France called Fortant de France. My eyes literally rolled to the back of my head. They pitched to us the urgent need for quality wines at a low price, and how this upcoming region would supply all our needs. We had to purchase 1,200 cases of this unproven entity because we were, after all, a loyal distributor of their products. We had just closed out 1,000 cases of the last unproven entity Vivache. Thank God I didn't have to do that one. Someone just should have found out if the Hammer or any of his boys had won a silver star.

The Jim rose to his feet and howled at our guests. Ironically, as all sides were engaged in pandemonium, it struck me that I was the only person in the room who had ever sold French country wines or really even knew what they were. So, in the hope of restoring some dignity to the meeting, I dispassionately told of my adventures and discovery of these wines and recommended that instead of putting them in restaurants as our guests had requested, that we purchase, say, a few hundred cases and put them in a high volumn, lower end grocery chain , a more appropriate place.

Now, both sides howled anew, and the Hammer dropped the hammer. He appointed as distributor for this area a fresh, new nepotist/amateur-owned company. End of meeting. To The Jim, this was a declaration of war. He had logged more hours just driving his golf cart, drinking Thunderbird and waiving his shotgun than this amateur/nepotist had spent in the business. And, by the way, he had bought and paid for his nice, cozy franchise and he didn't want it disturbed. Both sides traded nasty letters for several years, when suddenly the new nepotist/amateur sold his company. The Hammer called The Jim and the brand wound up in —you guessed it —in a high volumn, lower end grocery chain.

Through it all, there was one series of meetings and events that made it all worth it. The Wine Classic was the brain child of a local entrepreneur. He wanted to conduct a wine auction to raise money for public radio. I added while at the first meeting that a tasting event bringing the wineries and public together topped off with internationally famous wine celebrities would make it a major event.

All agreed, and we were on our way. The auction featured a bevy of local beautiful people about three sheets to the wind flailing their little bidding paddles as though they were batting down a nest of enraged hornets. But, as they say, it was all for a good cause.

Events such as these were special for two reasons: the public got to taste hundreds of wines —some great and rare —and the event featured the brightest stars in wine seminars. Kevin Zraly, the guru who orchestrated the Windows on the World restaurant wine list and wine school, was a clean-cut accountant-looking fellow, quiet in outward demeanor. But when he got on stage to do his talk, something clicked inside and he turned into the Mick Jagger of wine. He pranced, danced, strutted and thoroughly enthralled the audience. Kevin was fabulous as he seared his subject into your brain. There were also the usual glitches on the program. Dieter, our German wine boor, wanted more ice. Dieter wanted more room to display his wines. Dieter wasn't happy at all. Screw Dieter.

Our other stellar guest speaker was Clive Coates. He was a British Master of Wine, the highest form of recognized guru, and an author of countless definitive books on wine. We were lucky he had a moment to spare for us. Clive had an imposing girth and a full bristly beard. He possessed an outwardly gruff demeanor, but when seated beside several of the stunning local beauties over dinner, you could actually hear him purr.

Clive was our last major speaker of the day and I was looking forward to finally relaxing when I heard this strange sound emanating from a small room simultaneously holding another seminar. It sounded like "Yo mama, yo mama, yo mama," at a fast tempo. I opened the door slightly and there was our speaker Jim Stansberry, wine maniac and master coke-head, baked way beyond repair describing the elegant nuances of the pinot noir they were tasting using the two words "Yo mama" in a rapid series. He looked at me, calmed down a bit and switched to a softer, quieter "Yo mama." For some strange reason, his small audience completely understood.

After a week of meetings, seminars and general wine mania, Sunday was my downtime day. I was puttering around the house and flipped on 60 Minutes, a perennial favorite, when Morley Safer began talking about a phenomenon called "The French Paradox." It seemed they ate a world of fatty foods, but had much lower cholesterol than their American counterparts. We were seeing for the first that it was the red wine they were drinking along with their meals providing the health magic. My jaw dropped. Two words no one ever uttered together in wine mania were "wine" and "health" —now together for the first time in a sentence. We have finally overcome our national obsession with the demon alcohol. The French were getting their cardiovascular systems cleaned out with two glasses of wine a day.

The next day in the office, my phone rang continuously. The invisible wine guru stuck away in a nameless office in a distributor's warehouse became the new host of the wine-and-health information hot line. Every store that week was swept clean of all red wine. The 60 Minutes story of November, 1991, had ushered us into a new world. Ironically, the person who wrote more on the subject long before its publicity was my old friend from Montana, Gene Ford. He always was before his time, and his time was now. Red wine had in an instant replaced white as the wine of choice. The chief beneficiary of all of this was the merlot grape. It was soft and easy to drink for the amateurs now beginning their quest into wine mania.

In the middle inquiries about red wine, I got an unnerving call from my old guru from the days in Montana and Oregon, John Fraunfelder. I was on a complete high, and he was on an unfathomable low. The man, who had undergone both a lung cancer operation and a stomach cancer operation, returning to his full-time job after each, was sobbing uncontrollably. He was nearing his retirement from Seagram's when they fired him. Just like that. "I have no reason to get out of bed and put on my clothes. I can't even find a reason to put on my shoes." He was completely shattered in spirit. He died not long after our talk, a completely broken man.

I thought about the time I had him over for dinner years ago in Montana and opened my last bottle of the fabled 1955 Chateau La Mission Haut Brion with some rare lamb. He was overwhelmingly appreciative, telling me I should not have done something that great for him. After about a glass and a half his head nodded and his chin touched the front of his shirt. He wasn't drunk or even tipsy, just bone-tired from his never-ending travels.

While settling in one night a few years later, I chanced upon an article on John's old company in the Washington Post. Seagram's was rapidly moving into the entertainment business from their old standbys of wine and liquor. Senator Joseph Lieberman and William Bennett were presenting Seagram's with an award for aggressively edging out the competition in their distribution of the works of Marilyn Manson and Jerry Springer. This large salvaged manhole cover painted silver —the first ever Silver Sewer Award —was presented for their efforts in "connecting a large part of our citizenry to the sewer." It is a shame John wasn't around long enough to have presented them with the"Death of the Salesman " version of that award. Perhaps an old pair of bronzed shoes with a tie hanging down for appropiate placement in their board room.

The Gigantic wine distributor eliminated my position not long after John's death.

Layne and Judy got married.

Nick the Knife went out of business.

Stansberry died after a kidney transplant.

Frank died and his restaurant went out of business.

The Semi Jim got bigger and pinker.

Wine Buyer from Hell

After four years in corporate wine mania, it was time to re-invent myself. I took all of my suits and white, starched shirts, and dropped them off at Goodwill. I went out to shop for a new ride: the Anti-Ford Taurus. I found an edgy black Toyota MR2, so small it could barely hold a cup of coffee. It was a perfect ride for blasting Lou Reed over the stereo.

I found a retired ex-jock who needed someone to buy wine for a store he had just acquired. There are two types of wine buyers in wine mania: the docile, golf-playing, chumps-night-out freebie-loving, settle-for-mediocrity-because-you-don't-really-know-the-difference buyer. Then there is the wine buyer from hell. Wine buyers from hell are not necessarily mean, they're just demanding. No close-outs, no golf games, no dinners for the chumps; just a freshly opened bottle, a high-quality tasting glass and a notebook.

To be a wine buyer from hell, you have to have an edge. First, you set a goal of tasting a couple thousand wines a year and record your thoughts, scores and notions of each wine's price and quality. Take a close look at every vintage and memorize its qualities or lack of qualities. Anticipate trends; they'll get you ahead of the game. Look for gems others have missed. Look for hot, new producers. Don't be afraid to taste everything from every known grape variety and region, no matter how off the wall it may seem at first glance. And look 'em all up. Trust your tastebuds. The most important rule of all is to spit while tasting. Know when you are tasting the stuff, and when you are drinking it —and you will be OK. The wine buyer from hell tries to come up with new finds each week. That's what draws customers.

Identify the benchmarks for each grape, producer and origin and store all the info tightly in your head —it will come in handy.

Now for the tough part. About 20 salespeople from different distributors call on you each week. Some distributors are gigantic, and others fit in the palm of your hand. The number of companies stays pretty much the same, even as the gigantic ones gobble up the small ones and others just fall by the wayside to be replaced by newly created amateurs. Every city now has one or two gigantic distributors. It is amazing how each of the backs of their business cards has a series of printed platitudes saying how the customer is the end-all and be-all of their every breathing moment —that is, until you really need for them to take care of something.

One of my favorite gigantic distributors had just raised its prices with no notice, and on top of that had overcharged us by a couple thousand dollars. After a number of calls, to no avail, I took all of the company's bottles off the shelves, filling about 10 boxes, and stacked them in an ugly, unkempt pile. Then I pulled all of the shelf tags, shelf-talkers and signs, and crammed them into a large box behind the counter.

Somehow, a message reached the gigantic distributor's general manager to get over here pronto. This guy was attired head-to-toe in used-car slick, to the point of handing his little platitude card out to anyone within reach. His job, basically, was to listen to about a minute and a half of my howling, and launch into a heavily rehearsed Harvard MBA scripted dialog about how they were the gigantic end-all, be-all for their sorry little customers, and this occurrence was oh such a shame.

He was unfortunately accompanied by five managers from a very large, prominent winery. I asked him if he was completely finished. He was. I proceeded to pick up my weighty box from behind the counter, raise it in the air and dump its entire contents on counter, floor and them. I glared at them, dressed in my black on black and said, "I want my discounts and our money back, or those tags all over the floor are all you are ever going to see of your business in here." This is one of the harsher ways to hold your prices for your customers, but it is very effective.

That being said, the gigantic guys do manage to come up with some good stuff and occasionally a benchmark, although I wouldn't go so far as to say that many within their organization would know what one looked like. One such wine was the Kirralaa Bushvine Shiraz from Australia. At $15, it was one of the world's great bargain steak wines. The new brand was a Robert Mondavi-Rosemont collaboration loaded with black pepper, yet smooth as silk. Another one at that time was Chateau St. Jean's Sonoma County Merlot, which sold for $26. If the truth be known, I despise merlot. It's usually overcropped and made only with winery cash-flow in mind. This one was different. Loaded with bright cherry fruit, a fabulous middle palate and a memorable merlot finish, this is my merlot benchmark.

The complete opposite of the gigantic, well-rehearsed distributor was Roger, an amateur who owned a company that would fit in the palm of your hand. He was short, completely bald with a shiny chrome head, and wore an out-of-fashion blazer with a large gold crest. Roger could get away with all of this because he was English, and was clearly wine-selection wise a couple of years ahead of the curve. His forte was the wines of South Africa before South Africa even was remotely cool. The problem with being that far ahead and that small was that there was a good chance that you would tank. Roger tanked.

But before he went under he brought some very interesting wines around such as Chateau Libertas Cabernet Sauvignon from South Africa. At

$15, it was not a chateau, but did taste like a pre-70s Bordeaux. An exciting throwback to wine the way it was before globalization with an enticing taste of cabernet, sand and gravel. Kanankop Estate Cabernet Sauvignon from Stellenbosh was a $15 inventive, creative cabernet. Kanankop's pinotage, which is South Africa's local grape, is pretty cool as well. Try blending the two.

Given the soothing tones of Roger, I had to deal with personalities on the other side of the spectrum as distributor salespeople are invariably on the attack every buying day. Women have a tough time in wine mania, a world still largely populated by men. Carol represented the shrewdest of the species, the mind always working for her own gain. It never hurts to have a young Martha Stewart look and demeanor. She could flirt and be coy to get what she wanted, or be wildly bitchy when she didn't. For the buyer from hell, flirty, bitchy, batting eyelashes, and the occasional tantrum doesn't cut it. But the wines certainly did. She would have been better to let them speak for themselves.

One of those wines was the Macon Chantre Vielles Vignes from Domaine Valette at $17. You are not supposed to flip out over a humble white Burgundy, but this one is the buyer-from-hell's hot button. Its limestone earthiness provides the crunch and the old vines counter with a smooth, luxurious that rounds out the flavor. This one was a Macon benchmark.

Another of Carol's outstanding wines was a $12 Albarino from Valminor in Rias Baixas. This one was a wonder white from the Galacian region of Spain: smooth, transparent peaches in a glass. This is what summer tastes like. Don't forget to drink it while young as this is a fragile wine.

Every once in a while, an Olympic Gold Medal athlete of the salesperson genre descends on you. Stan the Man in no way resembles an athlete, being as wide as he is tall. At first glance, one is not terribly impressed with his twangy Southwestern Virginia accent. Stan does not cut an impressive figure, but he always brought me great undiscovered stuff. Stan the Man is an athlete whose every move I study.

In a market jam-packed with distributors of every stripe and ilk, most distributors find it difficult to out-think the Wine Buyer from Hell. They usually lack both the time and intellect. But Stan hits the road at 4 a.m., traveling from his hometown four hours away, and he's in my haunt by 7:30. He has been going over every nuance of his little talk with me for three and a half hours, honing it to perfection. Your taste buds are actually pretty alert early in the morning, even if your brain isn't. This lessens the chances of rebutting Stan the Man when he runs over you with spectacular wines and lists the reasons you simply cannot live without them. The passion and perseverance of wine maniacs like Stan the Man is what keeps many small wholesalers and their brands alive. The Wine Buyer from Hell enjoys being devoured by such a superior wine maniac.

One of Stan's best was the Patricia Green Pinot Noir from Oregon at $23. Patty Green grows and crafts wines of distinction in Newberg, Oregon. She is the winery equivalent of Stan the Man: she is relentless in her pursuit of those cherry and mushroom flavors you can only coax from the pinot noir grape. She too gets up at 4 a.m., but it's to work on her beloved vines.

A second from Stan was the Castel del Remei Gotim Bru, at $14. This one is new-wave Spain at its finest with its blend of local grapes done in an international style to make it a seamless red of complexity and fascination. If the Spanish had discovered this style of wine 25 years ago, California wouldn't exist. The discovery of a wine like this is worth a year's tasting through products.

On the other side of the counter are the customers. There is always one wine maniac who comes into your shop that, no matter how slimy he is, the Wine Buyer from Hell has to suck up to him. I call him the Trophy Wine Meister. When the right vintage aligns with the right amount of hype from the wine press, the Trophy Wine Meister reigns supreme. You can't get enough of these expensive wines.

All the devotees of these wines file through the door, from the cool to the comically absurd. They range from guy in the jogging outfit who knows the entire spectrum of collectables and makes brilliant, informed choices, to the one attired in the classic golfer outfit of white pants, white belt and fuchsia shirt. He has to have the newly anointed 94-point wine-press-rated Silver Oak Cabernet Sauvignon, which is of course sold out because of all the press. I recommended a fine bottle of Heitz Cabernet, a masterful substitute. The golfing geek wine amateur has never heard of this famous California producer, but is willing to reluctantly take my word, especially since he is buying four cigars, some plastic cups and a plastic corkscrew to take this great wine out to the golf course and murder it to impress his buddies. If you do cigars, do them with port. Also, if Joe Heitz were present witnessing this little trophy-hunting scenario, he would bash fuchsia boy senseless for killing his wine.

The Trophy Wine Meister also happens to be the local purveyor of chump's night out. Chumps night out is a free trip to a good local restaurant where you are plied with all the food and drink you desire. This is the primary way to entice wine buyers to momentarily lose their brains and purchase in mass quantity all the substitute wines when the trophy wines are gone. These third-rate, expensive, pseudo-trophy wines, after several glassfuls and mountains of free food, are supposed to taste pretty good.

Everyone loses at chump's night out because the pseudo trophy wines are usually overpriced, and the chumps are half-smashed when making that all-important buying decision. Only Trophy Wine Meister wins because there is no shortage of chumps. This is why those cheesy, inferior vintages wind up all over retail shops. In their own way, chumps really do have to pay for chump's night out.

That being said, the distributors who hold chump's nights out still managed to get out a few fabulous wines. One is, of course, the Silver Oak Cabernet Sauvignon from Alexander Valley at $80. Always one of the great cabernets, this one is luscious and delicious, without any edged. It is masterfully grown, well-crafted and aged to be enjoyed upon release.

Another one is Heitz Cellars Cabernet Sauvignon from Napa Valley at $75. This one is so chewy that it crunches. It's the benchmark for original Napa Valley Cabernets. With its big, ripe berries and no-nonsense flavor, try to keep this one away from plastic cups and cigars.

The strangest phenomenon for the Wine Buyer from Hell to deal with is the brand that becomes completely out of control, a mega-best seller. It also happens to be the one you tasted and dismissed as a piece of trash in a glass. I am of course referring to Yellow Tail Shiraz, with its cola-like flavor from beginning to end. To my tender sensibilities, it's sweet, syrupy, and the complete antithesis of wine —and millions of cases have sold.

What I did was put it alongside its contemporaries like Yalumba or Wolf Blass shiraz to see how it stacks up in a tasting. If you do this and still adore it, then keep sucking it up. Hell, you can even add ice cubes. This wine is more of a marketing study than a wine event. It is one of the first

Australian wines to boldly announce its nationality all over the label with that colorful kangaroo. With shiraz drinking at an all-time high and Australian wine on a roll, the Yellow Tail folks capitalized on a good thing. I still don't care for the wine.

The second wine sensation was, of course, Two Buck Chuck. The winery was founded by Charles Shaw, a banker amateur whose goal was to produce 12,000 cases of the world's finest gamay Beaujolais in Napa. Wrong. Napa is about cabernet, not Beaujolais. He went belly-up, and both the winery and brand name were purchased by Franzia, a major bulk-wine producer. Poor Chuck. It's one thing to have a cheesy wine named after you, but now there is an entire category to boot. The California wine industry has created the Extreme Value Varietal Category, or to put it not so politely, the Ultimate Recession Wine. To paraphrase a friend, "When you're out of Schlitz, you're out of money."

I mean, really, what do people think they're getting for two bucks? Not much. These are lifeless, soulless wines. They are the complete antithesis of wine. Being a Californian at heart, I have to wonder what people are thinking. The trend-setting wine drinkers of America just sucked up 81 million bottles of this stuff. Maybe the economy will improve, and these people will be able to afford better wine. I hope so.

On the other hand, there is always one person in wine mania who changes it all. People like this come to represent why you do what you do. Sherri and The Judge started out as customers who were really into Italian wine. They invited me to his office (the judges chambers, how cool is that?) to have a bite of pizza and a glass of their latest find. I had never had pizza with a judge.

Both were completely knocked out over Italian wine, and over each other. Sherri was a young lawyer, and her husband The Judge was ready to retire. They wanted to be Italian wine importers and sign up for a ride through wine mania. They brought out samples they picked up during their trips to Italy. The wines were just OK, and I issued the regulation warning about amateurs in the clutches of the tough wine mania world. Wine mania will cut you no slack, but The Judge's dream was to import Italian wine. The Judge had spoken.

I didn't see them for a while; they were off in the hills of Tuscany looking for better wines. It was too quiet. They had returned with new finds, when suddenly, The Judge had a heart attack and died. I didn't hear from Sherri for more than a year. One day, unannounced, she walked into the store with a valise full of wines and a business card bearing a picture of the Roman wine god Bacco. She was determined to live their dream. Her wines were sensational, selected with care. But she lacked several things an amateur needed: gobs of money and a couple of strong sales reps on a mission.

She lived the dream, going from amateur to full-fledged wine maniac, making a huge impression with her fabulous Italian wines. All the while, there was the threat of a dramatic currency change that would adversely raise her prices, a run of lousy vintages, and a severe economic downturn. She lived The Judge's dream through the finest years of Italian wine when, finally, all three importer's nightmares came to pass. She could hold on no longer and dissolved the company. The try was valiant and noble, and the wines were wonderful. She lived volumes about having guts and soul in wine mania. I miss her.

Italian wines have fine-tuned their art and have gone on a roll. One of the best I tried was Gini Soave from Veneto, at $15. Soave is probably the last wine that you look for today, but this light, almond-tinged and scented white danced in my glass. This is the classic example of why buyers should always try wines they otherwise wouldn't. Another great was the Cadalora Pinot Grigio, at $13. This was the benchmark for a quality pinot grigio at the right price. It drinks like elegant spring water. Consumers and buyers alike now drink so much pinot grigio almost accidentally that we really never get to know the grape.

Through it all, I found that being a tough and serious Wine Buyer From Hell saved me lots of time and unnecessary mistakes. Just listen, experiment and above all, taste.

Live on the Radio

It all began as a little lunch with a few people in the restaurant business and a guy who owned a local radio station. "Hey, why don't we do a live wine and food radio show," the radio guy said. Why can't I say no to stuff like this? I have thought about a thousand times both during and afterward. Just, "No." The fact that I had never done anything like this didn't slow me down. It just made it edgier and more exciting.

There I was the following Saturday morning, inside this crammed four-by-four booth, all geared up with earphones and a mike with an engineer on the other side of a thick plate-glass window. I guess I could just break the glass if I wanted to escape. The deal went like this: I sat down with a chef, his menu and his wine list, and we would banter live for an hour about what goes with what while answering phone calls from listeners.

The point of the finger from my engineer and the "Live on the air" sign really send adrenaline through you. The first couple of shows were pretty straightforward with the usual questions like, "What wine goes with bison?" "Why, Chateauneuf du Pape, of course." Asian chefs were the best because selecting wine for their food could be the most fun and entertaining.

Then it began to get weird. Ed, a supremely talented and supremely eccentric chef came on. He was wearing his usual attire, which I call The Scared Straight Motif, of a grungy sweat shirt without any trace of arms and the black Navy watch cap rolled up and pulled down tight. A nice little prison number, or perhaps it's the attire for spending months at sea.

"So, Ed," I began, "What menu items do you really enjoy doing?" He was dead silent, for what seemed like days. My engineer was flailing behind him, lip-syncing, "Dead air." We went to commercial.

I was ready to stab him with my homemade shiv when he finally spoke in a quiet, menacing voice. "What the hell do you like on the menu?" I immediately began to reel off everything he had listed including the frog's legs, the sweet breads and, yes, even the sheep's head. Of course, the sheep's head, was his personal favorite. We got out of there alive, though just barely. That was the moment when I knew the true meaning of the term "dead air." *We* were dead air.

The biggest horror in doing a live radio show was the last-second cancellation. I finally got into the habit of carrying tapes in my pocket, just in case. Some chefs choked after saying they would go on, and others had been on such a severe bender the night before they had no idea what day it was. Our best cancellation came when a major restaurant politely called and apologized that the chef too busy, but could they send a member of the staff instead? She showed up, petite and very cute, needing a hand with some trays outside. I dutifully lugged in all of this stuff covered in tin foil and hit the door about the time the "On the air" light went on. She was a patisserie who came bearing trays of just-made desserts and chocolates. We could barely talk throughout the show for stuffing those tasty morsels down our gullets.

Unfortunately, some shows had to put sponsors on the air. Frankly, I preferred to pick my own restaurants on account of the quality and consistency factors. Sponsors could downright flaky. However, one sponsor was noted for having the best Cajun food around, so having him on sounded like a good idea. The show fell on Halloween, my favorite dress up day. I went out and rented an outrageous matador's outfit, complete with tassels, ruffled shirt, funny hat and plastic sword.

I was the only person at the station, attired in my little Halloween outfit, when our guest appeared with the look of "I am completely appalled by all this" on his face. Our guest, as I was just discovering, was a major red neck. He clearly didn't care to sit in so cramped a space with a person wearing a head-to-toe matador's outfit. But once we began to talk about gumbo and okra and the great French wines that they went with, he stopped paying attention to my goofy little hat and it was a good show.

The real downside was visiting the sponsors incognito to see if they would either qualify or could stand up to the pressures of live radio. Most didn't. They were mom and pops with one manning the front of the house and the other in the kitchen, and both yelling at each other continually in dialect. Their food would invariably be quite good, and their wine list, or that folded envelope on the table that passed for being one, was crap. Every now and then the station owner would foist these people on me and it never was quite as bad as I had envisioned. There was always someone out there (a relative?) who was thrilled to talk to them live on the air.

All of a sudden the show was starting to become popular, with lots of call-ins and tons of questions for the chefs and me. The callers were energetic and opinionated. We liked it that way. Our piece de resistance show was that featuring Jimmy Sneed, a local chef with an international reputation. He resembled an oversized Gene Wilder with his hair going every where and his non-stop banter. I reminded him to bring his menu and wine list, because that was the theme of the program. As soon as he pulled up in front of the station and his kids began unloading the car, I knew I was in trouble.

They unloaded cooking utensils, Buntsen burners and boxes of food. We could barely move in our cubicle. We had just gone on the air, and I said, "Welcome to the wine and food show." Jimmy shouted, "Today it's the food show, and I'm cooking." The oil in the pan got hot and in went soft shell crabs, crackling and sizzling. My engineer and I panicked because directly overhead the sprinkler system was ready to unleash a torrent of water.

The phones lit up and it became "The Jimmy Show: All Jimmy All the Time." We were entranced by the soft shell monologue, followed by the proper seasoning monologue. Then this guy calls and asks about which chef's knife to buy, and we wound up with a major Jimmy discourse about the world's worst knives. One of those "world' worst knives" was pitched by our show sponsors in a commercial. My engineer and I were ready to commit hara-kiri with one of those knives.

There wasn't a moment I could relax during "The Jimmy Show"; the commercial times were especially exciting. One ad for one of the local sponsors came on and Jimmy leaped out of his chair in our tiny booth, swearing and screaming that the chef at that restaurant was a crook and a fraud. Not once did he mention his menu or wine list, which was the purpose of the show, but listeners got great live entertainment. The fresh, delectable soft shells were eaten after the show by my exhausted engineer and me.

The very next show features Jimmy's partner Adam. The front of the house man, Adam made the show as easy as Jimmy had made it painful. We went through their great dishes, effortlessly pairing them with their wines. It seemed this show lasted mere minutes while Jimmy's went on for days.

We were plagued with no-shows from chefs, and put together a final show as a favor for the station owner and one of his sponsors. They were a small mom-and-pop Italian restaurant in a strip mall. I checked it out first, and the place was surprisingly good. Their only request was to bring a few members of their staff as a thank you.

The day of show time, they tumbled out of the car about a minute before air time, with one woman still fumbling in the back seat. We were assembled in the cramped studio when in burst their final member, who was built like a Winnebago and carrying an accordion of similar girth. There was an ulterior motive for all of this. The owner promised his fledgling little group of musicians/staff members the opportunity to not only play, but to be heard live on the radio. Hence the sponsorship of the show.

The little band was really cutting loose for their cohorts in the mall. They were jumping, shaking and boogieing through a medley of Dean Martin favorites when we got a call. "What are you bastards doing down there?" I didn't know what "down there" meant. I just disconnected him and proceeded to listen to a loud and stirring rendition of Volare. Again, the caller, this time completely crazed. "I'm going to come down stairs and kill all of you people."

Ah, the station rented apartments upstairs to a whole group of generally pissed-off bubbas. Fortunately, we all managed to sneak out alive. In all, we did just under 100 shows, discussing many hundreds of dishes and their wine soul-mates. It actually was pretty fun work for an hour on a Saturday afternoon in wine mania.

Local Wine Journalist

The best thing about being fully settled into retail buying is the absence of those killer-long distributor meetings. You actually have time to spare. So, when the wine writer for the local daily newspaper quit, was dismissed, or left town, my interest was piqued. The paper needed a weekly freelance wine columnist: the local wine journalist.

I met with the paper's Food Editor Louis, and from her first sentence knew exactly what they were looking for: the wine version of the winner of Betty Crocker's World's Best Tuna Casserole Contest. Being the Wine Assassin was out of the question. To choose the columnist, the paper held a small competition among the local candidates. You were to write and submit two 500-word articles on the topics, "Inexpensive wines to have with grilled foods" and "Wines for a picnic". WOW! I'm becoming Betty Crocker. I won Betty's little contest, and Louis did dispense the best-ever advice for a free-lance writer. First, always know the paper can and will get rid of you any time it wants, and second, read The New York Times' food section every Wednesday to see how the pros do it.

Several weeks of wine and tuna-casserole type articles convinced me that this gig was going to be a real yawner. You set up a monthly writing calendar, assemble your wines to taste, and do your research. The only downside is sacrificing a good chunk of Sunday to write the following week's column. It is also no way to get rich.

Frankly, I was pretty bored by writing this crap when an e-mail arrived from New York. It was from Angelo Gajas' office asking if I would like to meet him in Washington, D.C. for an interview in a couple of weeks. Angelo Fucking Gaja! I dropped both Betty's book and the fine little tuna casserole I was working on. Angelo Gaja was the greatest living Italian wine maker.

The local rookie wine journalist —me —thought I would be part of a large group of reporters asking questions to the great man, kind of like a White House press conference. So, I studied up, reading every scrap of information I could find on Gaja. I had my five or so questions ready just in case I would get to ask one of them. What I completely failed to grasp in all my journalistic rookie ways was that this was a one-on-one lunch with Mr. Gaja himself. No help from the White House press corps.

I found myself standing toe-to-toe with the great man in the lobby of the Willard Hotel in D.C. This is without a doubt the coolest person I have ever met. Picture James Dean at the age of 60. He is six feet tall, 200 pounds, and wearing Italian-made comfort clothes that fall naturally on his frame. He has a chiseled face and a brushed-straight-back head of hair. His voice matches his persona: cool and slow with a smooth Italian accent. This man knows exactly who he is and carries with him the charisma and guru-like quality of a person who took over the family winery when Italian wine was in the dumps, and elevated it to the major world-class place it is in today.

We sat down for lunch and tasted his famed single vineyard Barbarescos —at $250-$350 per bottle .They were complete balance and perfection. He shared his vision of making his native region a great and important land for wine, along with his ideas for his upcoming projects. The greatest insight he imparted was his fanatic notion on how to pick the estate's grapes. He worked for seven years in the vineyard before his father would let him make wine. The theory he developed was to go over every centimeter of land and inspect every bunch of grapes, discarding in the field everything of inferior quality. Then he attacked the barrel situation, buying wooden staves, air-drying them for long periods, and having his own coopers make them to fit his specifications. Meanwhile, his neighbors reused their worn-out clunkers for decades.

You could taste this care in all of his wines. He not only revitalized his local region of Barbaresco, but also brought Italy into the modern world. I had just shared thoughts on wine mania with one of the all-time greats. I got home and wrote this fabulous piece on the guru Gaja and his wines. My food editor hated it. It wasn't really what she was looking for, blah, blah, blah. So I crawled back to Betty Crocker Land and knocked off a few token inspirational pieces on the sublime qualities of wine and barbeque.

The columns were rolling every week when —boom —somebody tore the guts out of a really good piece by chopping it in half and sticking the remainder beside a picture and article of a NASCAR tailgate party. It was done by —you guessed it —my editor. I knew Gaja was considered highbrow, and Betty Crocker was just right, but where does a NASCAR tailgate party piece fit in? I would now be fighting both Betty and Bubba for my little space.

Ironically, interviews began rolling in around that time. Good interviews. Strong interviews. What was most intriguing about these interviews was they involved people I knew from my Oregon and California days who were reinventing themselves. Gaja clearly was not. He was reinventing his birth place. What about everybody else?

Denis Cakebread brought new releases of his wines from the family winery in Napa. They were all wines to drool over. Their winery had attained Trophy Hunter status, and you could either collect them or murder them in a plastic cup on the golf course. His chardonnay, sauvignon blanc and cabernet sauvignon were at the very top of their form.

Jack, father and head of the family, led the operation from its automotive garage in Oakland to Napa, and everyone assumed their places in the family work effort. The family members had convincingly reinvented themselves. Father Jack; cook, author and wife Dolores; and Dennis the winemaker. There was no slow-down in sight as winery people kept streaming in.

Michael Havens of Haven's Wine Cellars was low key, but the more he talked about himself and his background, the more I was knocked over by the fact that he was the genuine article. He was the man who had really reinvented himself. He had a lively laugh, and was attired head-to-toe in one form or another of Birkenstock. He was the laid-back English professor, the sophisticated proto beatnik who looked like he built his own cabin in the Napa Valley. He quit a university teaching position to attend wine school at U.C. Davis. Havens was the merlot grape —that cash cow of wine —into an entirely different world. He was shaping it from a sorry little one-note samba most wineries were turning out en masse to a string quartet with lush tones and complexity. Michael Havens was the ideal wine maniac, tackling something that was uphill and out of reach in a pair of Birkenstocks, and succeeding.

After dealing with Betty and Bubba as companions for a year or two, and not forgetting that magical dose of the New York Times every Wednesday, I began to notice a pattern to writing a weekly wine column. There were the regular tuna casserole pieces (Pinot Grigio and its new-found popularity), the bigger picture (Italy takes on the world), and interviews.

Then there are of course the prerequisite seasonal articles (Valentine's Day, Thanksgiving, etc., etc.)

The most important question, make that dilemma, for the local wine journalist is that of hype. When is it news and when is it hype? The arrival of a great vintage is always news, but the breathless call to go out and chase down every last bottle can be the worst kind of hype. Especially when that same journalist has tasted from those barrels and knows there may be something just as good coming along soon. The journalist is usually several steps ahead of the wine buying public. This can either be very good or very bad. Also, people like those pyrotechnic filled columns far better than the ordinary ones.

The strangest and most peculiar hype was that related to the Millenium. It called forth every form of nut and quasi nut case on the planet, not to mention an entire host of computer nerds acting as prophets. I wrote about the wine choices for the Millineum until I nearly dropped, and then one thing dawned on me about a year afterward: the vast majority of people who went out and spent a pile of money on those expensive Champagnes didn't have a clue about what they had just shelled out the equivalent of a monthly car payment for.

Then, when Champagne sales fell at the time they should have risen, it all became apparent. Too many people had spent far too much money on something that they didn't understand. With wine you begin in the middle and work your way up to the top after a few years, so that you can appreciate why you have just shelled out so much money on that single bottle. At the end of it all the wine maniacs made a short-term gain resulting in complete long-term popular confusion. So much for hype.

The best local story is the one that you have to work your way into. The local Greek festival is that kind of an event. I figured that since they sell Greek wine there, an article would be a fun piece. I called the organizers and got the same reception you would give the Secret Service if they banged on your door at two o'clock in the morning. Talking with a friend who belonged to the local Greek church hosting the event, I was reminded that these people were a very clannish bunch and not easy to get to know. They reluctantly set up a bizarre meeting. Twenty male church elders around a table, all nervous as cats, ready to bolt or leap. The tension in the room let me know that these folks did not feel comfortable with outsiders, especially one with a notebook and pen in his hand.

Prior to my meeting with elders, I read a couple of books on Greek food and one (I think there is only one) on Greek wine. As we were sitting, staring at each other, I began to speak of some of my favorite Greek dishes and their local, indigenous wines. Forty eyes got really wide. The main elder clapped loudly and out came platters of steaming hot food and bottles of chilled wine.

We dug in, talking and comparing the local member's favorite dishes and wines. They were experiencing what they loved and gleeful to share it with their new journalist friend. Always study, always come prepared. When the article appeared, it more than did the food, the wine and the event justice. The elders invited me back next year to help them evaluate their wines and throw down a stuffed grape leaf or two.

Another lesson I learned was to read everything. While reading the Washington Post, a curious piece popped up in the obituaries. It was an obit on the father of my winemaker friend Archie Smith II. The piece bowled me over. I knew Archie Sr. was a hard-working winery owner, but had no clue he had been a Marine combat pilot in WWII on Guadalcanal. After some digging, I turned this news bit into a Veteran's Day article on four wine maniac patriots. The first was Phillip Mazzei, grape grower and colleague of Thomas Jefferson. He left Monticello to join the local revolutionary militia, and was eventually sent to Europe to help assist the cause by raising money on the continent for beleaguered troops. For his efforts, Jefferson presented him with one of five original copies of the Declaration of Independence.

Our second was Alexis Lichine. He was born in Russia, became a naturalized American citizen and served with Ike as a military intelligence officer in WWII. After the war, he wrote some of the finest books on wine for Americans and wound up owning several Bordeaux chateaux. Our third, Jack Eckstein, was a local grape grower who served as a Navy fighter pilot in Viet Nam. My favorite was the last: the unassuming bed and breakfast owner and worker/purveyor of a fine vineyard Peter Sushka. Peter was a diesel submarine commander during Viet Nam.

When not scouring for ideas, there was always the constant bombardment of e-mail, phone calls, press releases, and Fed Ex letters —not to mention the gigantic winery frantically sending a 40-page e-mail on the update of its mediocre vineyard, where they produce a few million cases of its mediocre wine. Through this barrage, I kept my eyes and ears on one winery in particular: Gallo. They were a slow to move as an elephant, but when they did it was always worth checking out why.

A contact from Gallo asked me if I would like to interview one of their people about the winery's new Sonoma County wines. You bet. Gallo had taken a huge leap forward in quality since my Montana days and were headed in a whole new upscale direction. They booked a small banquet room at a local Holiday Inn. I sat in the lobby expecting the march of the troops.

In came the five or so young trench-coated disciples I had come to know so well. We were then joined by five people from Gallo's local distributor. Their winemaker was a mystery altogether.

The Gallo army didn't let me down, however, because smack in the middle of the boys sat a wizened, stooped, older gentleman somewhere in his eighties. "Dr. George Thoukis, Vice President and Senior Winemaker of the Gallo Winery, at your service," he said with a courtly bow. This was, I said to myself, going to be a trip. I could have gotten any number of protégés, but as luck would have it, I got the man himself.

"Would you like to taste our wines?" he asked with an impish look. "Hell no," I said. "I want to find out your background and who you are." His little entourage tightened up. This wasn't part of the official script. He was real, all right. U.C. Davis class of 1953. He experimented with chardonnay as a winemaker for Gallo in the 1950s, which was long before anyone drank chardonnay. He led Gallo's wine-making team, tasting 20 or so different wines a day, every day, from all over the world. He put together the Sonoma project over a 20-year period.

This was Gallo's guru. They ordered my lunch while everyone else ate, and they boxed it up for me when they were done. George Thoukis was one of these rare people in wine mania who saw it all, knew it all, and lived it all.

All 12 of us tasted his wines. By the time we finished this exercise, all our eyes were open wide —even the little dudes in their trench coats. The Gallo of Sonoma wines were clearly wines someone had thought about and labored over for a long period of time. They were selling at around $10, and delivered more than your money's worth. The chardonnay had a good touch of oak, and the Dry Creek zinfandel had that brambly raspberry quality the grape is famous for. "How long have you been drinking and making zinfandels Dr. Thoukis?" was my last question. He looked up, looked around, and said, "Forever."

In another fascinating piece, I got wind of a wine-maker change at Chateau St. Jean. This was an event that seldom occurred at this winery, and the press agents were taking the new show on the road to ensure their fanatic customer following stayed intact and that the wine press maniacs were happy with the new winemaker. They were too high-profile to stumble.

The interview for this story wasn't the local Holiday Inn with a soup-and-sandwich special. No. This was going to be top-drawer all the way. We met in a private dining room suite in the best hotel in town. Lemon slices came in the water and hot towels arrived for dainty fingers. Dinner was destined to be chump's night out in overdrive.

Through all the pleasantries, warm finger-bowls and making nice-nice, I become convinced that somewhere in all of wine mania I have met this newly anointed winemaker for hallowed Ch. St. Jean. We circled and sniffed and both said, "Oh, my God, the bad old days in Virginia." I knew Steve Reeder when he was winemaker at the doomed Dominion Wine Cellars. This was a place with too many growers, most of whom couldn't make it past amateur on the wine-maniac food chain.

We talked about old places and times, and it became clear to me that his resume was a tribute to sheer guts and will power in wine mania. Of course his wines were good —damn good. He had lived in wine-making hell holes and was now in the land of carte blanche as a wine maniac. He had both the tools and the talent. The next year he won the No. 1 wine in the world title from The Wine Spectator. No one ever deserved it more.

While my columns weren't being sliced up to make room for NASCAR, my editor was demoted to staff writer. At the same time, local writers were being knocked off one-by-one and replaced with news wire copy. This is a newspaper's version of outsourcing. I found it peculiar because the Betty Crocker stuff sent across the wire was more innocuous than the stuff written by the now-defunct locals. The highlight of my wine writing week was reading the New York Times to see if my article had kicked their veteran guru wine writer Frank Prial's butt.

Aside from all the tasting, research and general perusing of the written world of wine mania, it was always good to have hot sources. One phoned me and said, "Something is going on at Monticello. Call them now." Nothing wine-wise had happened since Jefferson died, and even he never made wine there, much as he always wanted to. I called my old friend Gabrielle Rausse, now a gardener at Monticello. He planted vines using Jefferson's chosen varieties, trellising and 18th-century methods, and had managed to make the first wine ever at Monticello. I immediately dropped everything I was doing and headed to see him.

While waiting for Gabrielle in the gift shop at Monticello, the room was buzzing. The entire staff was in high wine mania. CNN picked up the story and all types of people were jetting into the tiny Charlottesville airport in private planes to pick up bottles. The wines were referred to as cultural artifacts.

The best part of the story (apart from beating Frank Prial to it) was standing with Gabrielle in Jefferson's vineyard at Monticello as Jefferson would have experienced it in the early morning with fog rolling in. On one side was Monticello, with its architectural purity and on the other, the mountains with their ruggedness. What an exquisite feeling. Gabrielle and I tasted wine from the barrel in a winery that was about the size of a large coat closet. Everything was done as it would have been in the 18th century. What an exquisite story.

The biggest problem with being the local wine journalist, apart from the crappy pay, the tuna casserole mentality and NASCAR muscling into your space, was reading big-time wine critics flailing local wine writers, saying they lack a backbone because they don't criticize anyone. We are viewed as freebie-loving chow-hounds who suck up to wineries. In defense of the local wine journalist, on his best day he gets to publish about 750 words —the size of a sheet of postage stamps. It makes sense to do a story on what you liked with such a miniscule space. If you have a couple of pages to work with, criticism is easy. Also, try running a Freedom of Information Act request past your editor and watch her bolt for the door on an urgent errand.

There was one story that sent every local wine journalist out on the chase. Robert Parker, esteemed wine critic and publisher of The Wine Advocate newsletter, unleashed a whirlwind of bad press in his yearly review of California wines on Dec, 23, 2000. It wasn't so much his analysis of the greed-ridden 1997 vintage ("Show them the Money"), as it was his over-the-top unfavorable review of the Robert Mondavi Winery.

Parker is a lawyer by training who can state his case boldly. "In 22 years I have never been more distressed as well as perplexed by evaluations of a particular winery than those that follow." This was looking to be a winery killing piece, even with the God-like status of Mondavi in the eyes of wine maniacs and consumers. "To my way of thinking, [these are] indifferent, innocuous wines that err on the side of intellectual vapidness over the pursuit of wines of heart, soul and pleasure." The only way to fairly cover this would be to continue writing weekly columns while tasting

Mondavi wines over a several month period. Also, to give the Mondavi winery due justice, its wines, per the Mondavi philosophy, had to be tasted alongside food.

After a month of tasting, experimenting and serious thinking, my conclusion was that we Americans are too carried away with the flavors of overblown, oversized wines. Along with the Mondavi wines, I tasted a variety of California's finest, including those by the famed Turley Wine Cellars. We have shaped our taste buds to coincide with the SUVs we drive. Finesse and delicacy are seldom in our vocabularies any more.

My article wound up being the usual 750 words, but it was a tightly reasoned essay on wine and food: what works and what doesn't. Robert Mondavi's wines were perfection with the right dishes. The classic examples were Oysters Rockefeller with Mondavi's Stags Leap 1999 Sauvignon Blanc. A more powerful wine eliminates the delicate play of flavors in this dish (Parker thought the wine too subtle). Crabcakes and Mondavi 1999 Napa Chardonnay (a wine that Parker found unexciting by itself) brought out the complexity of the dish and operated in absolute harmony. I found a great maturity of purpose in these wines. In the weekly regimen of writing, one rarely gets the opportunity to take a long look at a project.

Every few days, I check incoming mail. Among the usual stack of press releases was a letter from the Robert Mondavi Winery. This one lacked the standard white address sticker. Inside was a letter written by Robert Mondavi saying that he had read my article. "I have traveled the world over to understand what the ultimate purpose is in wine. I have been in the business since 1937, 64 years, and our family has come to the conclusion that wine should be friendly, gentle, have layers of flavor and harmonize with food. Your article brings out beautifully and simply our belief in what wine should be —congratulations. Sincerely, Robert Mondavi." For a local wine journalist, it doesn't get any better. The letter was followed by a one-on-one interview with the guru's guru himself.

Being a freelancer, I seldom visited the newsroom. On the few times I did, I figured there had been a lot of journalistic outsourcing going on. There weren't many writers around. Also, I noticed that the paper contained fewer and fewer stories from local writers and more wire-service copy. It felt like the paper was prepared, freeze-dried and shipped to the market from some distant place. It resembles a tight local package, but really has little relation to where you live.

The entire food section was eventually outsourced, with the exception of my old editor occasionally writing a piece on the foods of NASCAR or a Betty Crocker Tuna Casserole Contest. When everything is outsourced, there is no writing synergy, no interaction. Everything is flat, like the Betty Crocker story version of Moroccan meat balls (that won't scare the kiddies). I pictured a faux Moroccan Betty Crocker, with a politically correct dab of henna, holding up a casserole dish filled with her non-offensive meatballs. So much for local food and wine writing in America.

I signed on as a freelancer to a local arts, entertainment and restaurant review publication. Fewer articles, less work, but a greater sense of freedom. My turf expanded to wine-list reviews, restaurant criticism, and food and wine articles. With the new job came liveliness in the air that replaced the odor of journalistic job death. More weekly food and arts papers should seek emerging talent in food and wine writing. Hold Betty's little contest again, but with sushi instead of tuna casserole.

While working retail as my day job, I spoke to many a wine wannabe strutting his stuff in wine chat rooms with the cast of poseurs. These are the types who should write 750 words every week. It will give them a taste of what they're made of in wine knowledge, and expand it beyond their wildest dreams. The pay is low, but if you persevere, you can make it from amateur to maniac. And maybe, if you work hard enough, you'll get the opportunity to sit wine-glass to wine-glass and interview the gurus. That in and of itself is enough to keep local wine journalism alive.

The Judge and the Jury

One thing you don't realize when you sign up to be the local wine journalist is that there will be a host of people coming at you from all directions, asking for lots of things. One of the most aggressive, loaded for bear, groups (apart from wineries themselves) are organizers of wine competitions. Think about it. The right gold medal or best in show award at the right place and time can bring instant fame and fortune. The problem for the winery and the gold-medal shopper is not all wine competitions are created equal. Far from it. I have experienced three types of wine competitions, which I have nicknamed after their judge's attributes.

1. The Wine Maniacs
2. The Chump's Night Out
3. Would You Pass that Vinaigrette to have with my Chateau Lafite, please?

The Wine Maniacs

The first and most important thing the gold-medal shopper needs to ask is "Who are the judges?" They don't have to be stellar names or gurus — though that sometimes helps —but they do have to follow some form of wine mania. Winemakers, journalists, wine buyers, distributors, they all add up to a group of people who judge knowing the deliberation and toughness that goes with choosing wine medals. The variety of styles in judging ranges from tasting and dropping your selections in a ballot box to be analyzed by a computer to tallying each vote by a show of hands.

A wine judging can be as calm and soothing as a day at the beach or a fierce shouting match with a group of puffed, cuffed and stuffed outsized ego maniacs. I've experienced both. A good head judge sets the rules and criteria and keeps order. Sometimes the competition is tightly monitored, while other times the head judge resembles a hockey referee with his hands in his back pockets observing the blood and mayhem.

Dr. Bruce, a fine head judge, laid out one of the best sets of criteria to not only keep the peace, but to give all of the wines their due. Wines should be judged on their intensity, vitality, purity, complexity, subtlety, strength, length and balance. Just tattoo all of those words on your forearm and wine judging will be a snap. Think of each of these things while tasting your next glass of wine, then multiply that by 1,200 and you've got it.

A usual competition will have 300 to 1,200 or so wines laid out in flights of 10 wines each. Each flight will be the same grape variety or wine type. It all sounds simple until you raise your hand with your medal score and announce your thoughts to the other judges.

During one memorable competition, while judging a bunch of fairly innocuous $6 chardonnays, I mentioned liking one in particular because it had a more flavor than its tasteless companions. A nationally acclaimed wine writer judge drove both his boots into my face because I had pressed his hot button. He growled and snapped, "This wine was no doubt made by using an immersion of oak chips" instead of being aged in the sacrosanct oak barrel. As the head judge separated us I cried out "Hell. For $6, I don't care if it was aged in a pig bladder."

We eventually made it all the way to dessert wines without causing anyone (including ourselves, undue harm when the NAWWJ (nationally acclaimed wine writer judge) leaped to his feet in complete admiration over a little East Coast dessert wine. He billed, cooed and genuflected. I could taste only the more than propped up flavors made by the wine maker deep freezing bunches of ho-hum grapes, not the serious late-harvest stuff left hanging on the vine for the entire harvest. You simply remove water and concentrate the flavor, which provides the illusion of a true late-harvested wine. I sat back through all of his cooing and added "You wanna talk about a phony technique, this is it: the Golden Popsicle. Except that the oak chip technique has been substituted for G.E. (General Electric) and you get to pay $40 instead of $6. Not all phony techniques are created equal." After we wrung each other's necks for a few minutes, the head judge pulled us apart.

Wine judging is physically exhausting, and if they are right-on, very rewarding. If you have decided it all fairly, and have worked up the energy to get in a blind rage or two over what you believe is right, then you can rest assured those gold medals really mean something.

My all-world wine judging team (with some members you have heard of, some you haven't) would consist of the wisest, fairest, cleverest and baddest of all judges. The art form distilled to its essence.

Warren Winiarski of Stag's Leap Wine Cellars. Legend has it that he received the news that he had just won the Paris Tasting, putting himself and California wines forever on the map, while making sales calls to try and place his fledgling brand. He never had to make a sales call again. Sitting beside this man in a wine judging is akin to studying Eastern religion with the Buddha. He smoothly climbs into the inner workings of the wine, taking it all apart and weaving it back together before your eyes. The coarsest, most jaded ego-driven judge gives Warren his due.

Wilfred Wong, a retail guru from California, shows up looking like he is attending a week-long Microsoft convention, complete with leather satchels and canvas bags piled in front of him, filled with a number of laptops. When he sets up to judge the wines, his stuff is sprawled everywhere. He not only records his own comments but yours as well. He has decades of tasting notes on discs stuffed into those bags. The first time you see him with all of that stuff, you are disconcerted, and when he moves it into action, you are stopped cold. The next judging, you simply ask, "Wilfred, what did I say about that wine last year?" He will know.

Dan Berger, wine writer for the L.A. Times and a zillion other pubs, is cranky and obstinate; a freight train among judges, but one of the greats. Among the top piss-off distractions wine judges do is a little number called "stop the competition." Any judge can stop the competition cold for any reason. Usually it is because they believe they taste a defective bottle. In actuality, it has the same disruptive effect as stopping a train. Dan stops competitions a lot.

I always set aside the supposed offending glass to compare it with the freshly opened one, or in other words, to test the judge. Corked wines are the leading offender in "stop the competition." It is a contaminated cork that renders a wine useless in flavor and smelling of old cardboard. Checking behind Dan's corked wines is checking behind the master, albeit a cranky and obstinate one. He separates differences that are so minute that his nose should wind up in the Smithsonian some day for further study.

Michael Franz, Washington Post wine writer. There can be a certain feeling among the non-wine-drinking public that what we do is for wimps: swirling, sniffing and spitting into delicate spittoons. One look at Michael Franz in action will dispel those thoughts. He resembles Bill Wyman, bass player for the Rolling stones. Michael Franz gets down, attacking the wines in full frontal assault. By the time he gets done checking it all out you are convinced. This guy is one persuasive wine maniac.

Ann Burda, wine writer from Washington, D.C. She sits erect, wearing her wine judging game face and is a tad kinder and gentler than Michael Franz, but not by much. Because they are an emerging force and a minority in wine mania, women judges put greater effort into sorting it all out and expressing themselves. The people of wine mania wine judging are tough, they take no prisoners, and their medals count for something. Each one can mean a thoughtful discussion or an all-out tussle in the rink.

The Chump's Night Out Wine Judging:

This type of judging is usually conducted by a group of people whose major desire is to promote themselves, their city, civic organization, or a fund-raising cause. The dead giveaway here is the thick dispersal of local doctors, lawyers and captains of industry cleverly foisted off as wine judges.

These people may enjoy playing the role of wine judges. I may very well be qualified to perform open heart surgery, but I'm not, and they aren't qualified to judge wines. There are always enough wine maniacs in any given area to can step forward, hold a judging, and give out quality medals. Get a hold of the event brochure, look at the back page listing the judges, and if they aren't wine maniacs, bag it and move on to looking at medals in another competition. The chump's night out is still the chump's night out, albeit a group of better-dressed and well-heeled chumps.

Would You Pass That Vinaigrette to Have With My Chateau Lafite, Please?

This is a judging that has one express mission: to pass out as many medals (golds, naturally) as possible. They will hang from every bottle in every tasting room and at every festival. The winery staff will proudly proclaim that these gold medals synonymous of the highest achievement were won at the "International Lint Festival and Wine Competition."

This type of competition is set up as an innocent affair by a civic organization, region or a wine group, all with a vested interest in creating local or regional excitement. The organizers make their money by charging a fee for each wine entered. It is a lucrative enterprise based on the amount of interest generated and fueled by the number of medals been handed out. A good rule of thumb, after checking the presence or lack thereof of wine maniacs, is to carefully look at the number of medals awarded. There should be a few golds, a few more silvers and a host of bronze. If there are 1,200 wines entered and 1,000 medals given, head for the nearest exit.

Other judges are instrumental in creating interest, excitement and general mayhem in the wine maniac scene. Above and generally beyond the honest hard-working irascible wine judge is what I am fond of calling "The 90-point Wine Blessing." This is bestowed with great fanfare by the Wine Spectator and Robert Parker in The Wine Advocate.

The 90-point Wine Blessing is such a momentous event that wineries have been known to jack their prices out of logical proportion, wholesalers to dole out the blessed commodity to only their most subservient and loyal customers, and retailers to both raise the price and sell it in hushed and guarded tones. The entire point system works like a judging except it eliminates judges and reduces your playing field down to the two magazines mentioned above.

That being said and done, there is no lack of enthusiastic feeding frenzy for any wines that score 90-plus points. Unfortunately, this system has so carried the day in the minds of wine drinkers and collectors that anything below 90 points sounds the death knell of absolute boredom to the wine-interested. For my money, the best values have been hidden away in those 85-87 point wines. As a wine judge, these merit solid silver awards, and in a wine judging they do create a level of excitement.

The 100-point system first emerged in the Wine Advocate by Robert Parker. It replaced the scholarly 20-point system created by the University of California at Davis. The 100-point system started out well enough but with the evolution of the probability of big winery bucks based on a big blessing, the wines have become predictable. Let's face it, a 90-point score has always been sexier than a 20-point one, or for that matter, 18.5 points.

I like to picture the big 100-point wine blessing like this. The food critic of the New York Times anonymously walks into a restaurant. The problem though is that all the staff already knows who he is and what he likes. The owner goes back into the kitchen and tells the chef and the chef promptly begins to prepare the critic's favorite dishes. Out they come, thrilling the food critic, who promptly begins writing down scores from 90 to 100 points. Then, of their own volition, they turn into the signature dish of the restaurant. Want it or not, you'll be having it sooner or later.

Those 90-point blessing wines are beginning to look, smell and taste very similar. Winemakers, like chefs, are not stupid. They notice when the words fat, voluptuous, unctuous, ripe, rich, thickness and on steroids occur next to wines with 90-plus blessings. It's like walking into that restaurant unannounced, but everyone knows who you are and the dishes have your name on them. They are certainly tasty, but they are all the same.

One of the alltime most frustrating experiences in the great '90 Point Plus' dance is that held yearly by the Wine Spectator Magazine- their Top 100 wines of the year. Having been both a wholesaler and retailer your life spins out of control when this thing comes out every year. It is during the holiday season (The 60 Days of Wine Mania), which is bad enough, but the trophy envy for those top ten reaches epic crazed proportions. Can you spell unattainable? After all, those are a mere 100 of all the wines that are on the planet, or so it seems. The smart collector and saavy consumer who buys into this system and follows the Wine Speculator should set aside a monthly sum and chase the 90 plus point wines while they are still chaseable. This is the time moments before they sell out and leave you panting on my doorstep every December. Or you could just bag it all and select the wines that you like.

The esteemed wine writer Matt Kramer has picked up on what is occurring with the sexiness of those 90 point wines and has chosen to call it "The low cut dress syndrome." The wine version of the Versace evening dress entering the room wins, garnering market success and critical acclaim. This is all heady and amazing stuff, especially after these wines endure thousands of tastings, judgings, and ceremonial dances with medals.

Based on current wisdom (?) surrounding the 90-point and above blessing, Pamela Anderson could do to Napa what she had done to herself. Just purchase a nice little vacuum concentrator and a reverse osmosis machine that removes excess water from grapes. All she has to do is to bottle her deep, dark, rich wine, put a picture of her bursting out of the label holding some cabernet cuttings and call it all Napa Cabernet Implants.

I guess I have learned one thing over the years judging wine and that is to keep an open mind. Judge a wine based on what it is, not on what your personality wants it to be. Again, as I look down at this these words tattood on my arm, all the answers are clear: Intensity, Vitality, Purity, Complexity,

Subtlety, Strength, Length and Balance. No where does it say anything about steroids, low-cut dresses, or wines that have to taste the same.

Teacher with a Glass

In the late 1980's, one of my friends decided to move to Paris, live in Monmartre, and travel around in one of those armadillo cars looking for wines to export. He left me with a handful of his favorite wines and dragged me in to pinch hit as teacher of his wine class at the University of Virginia. After a long day in wine mania, the last thing that I wanted to do was a little dog and pony show for a bunch of college kids. I had taught the half-hour " Name the label and let's learn how to open the nice bottle of wine" for a bevy of restaurant people over the years, but a two hour lecture wine class was a different creature altogether.

After about three minutes, it became apparent that the students were not only bright, but they were also into it. They couldn't move their fingers around their laptops fast enough, such was their enthusiasm. All had been to Europe, and all were bursting with energy to learn about wine.

I quickly changed my mind about this little show. This actually looked like fun. I would put together what I would want to learn if I was starting from scratch- a "Wine Scratch 101 class". First, I required the students to bring their own glasses. This held down the cost and provided a humorous forum on what to avoid. The Jimmy Buffett series is great for margueritas but lousy for vino.

I threw in a couple of fine show and tell exhibits from home. Those ultra-thick, ornately carved two-pound crystal goblets are perfect for entertaining heads of state, but ideal for killing aroma and flavor. Put them on e-Bay right now. The best deal on quality glasses- at least for this stage of the game- is the kind worth scouring from Pottery Barn to Pier One, the reasonably priced hand-blown European glasses. These give a true sense of aesthetics, a feel for quality on a student's budget. They're lightweight and irregular, as befits a handmade product.

We then would line up ten different glasses with the same wine, and select a lucky student to step forward, taste, and explain the differences to all of his classmates. This is a dramitic learning experience, complete with gasps of disbelief when the fabulously expensive, ornately carved clunker gets massacred by a Romanian hand blown glass coming in at a whopping $2.00 a stem.

The big boys of the glass world are the mighty Riedel and the slightly less mighty Spiegelau, both masters of European glassware. I am constantly experimenting between tasting wine in glasses made by each of these two producers, with their various and sundry styles and shapes. Reading Matt Kramers book Making Sense of Wine, 2nd edition set me on a mission to compare the rest of the glass world to his all-time favorite multi-purpose glass: the Riedel Chianti Classico (Vinum series) # 416/15, which runs around $22.00 a stem. The company also call this glass the Sangiovese, Zinfandel, and Montepulciano, it is one of the great stems in all of wine mania. My number's two and three picks are the Spiegelau Grande white wine at$12.00 and their Burgundy Grande, also at $12.00.

The 80's were an era of the rebirth of popularity of French wine. "All French, all the time" as friends and I jokingly referred to it. Even wine regions that weren't vaguely like France were trying their best to offer themselves as suitable in both style and taste —the French knockoff. The operative word in class was "Terroir", flavor of place, or influence of soil and region on the flavor of the grape. We managed to delve into miniscule regions, experiencing unknown grape varieties, and viewing photos of the real peasants who had no teeth.

I led the class charge in looking for that unique something in wine until you found it. We tasted classic Macon wines that sucked the limestone out of the ground, Pouilly Fuisse that reeked of gravel, Chateauneuf du Pape that was crawling with those big stones of the region, and Chablis, whose ancient oyster skeletons you had to crunch through. We waded through that thing called "Terroir" with abandon.

Then the trends changed. In just a few short years the wine scene focus shifted to chardonnay. Big, oaky, meaty, gutsy, overblown and overripe chardonnay. It was to be chardonnay for brunch, lunch and dinner, followed by a little chardonnay nightcap. The exciting thing about it all was that it was diametrically different from France, so the curriculum had to be redrawn to include a "Welcome to Oak" chart listing everything from the miniscule green apple flavor with a slight, bare hint of oak to the mighty muffin oozing with hot buttery flavor, and every winemaker's oak fantasy inbetween.

Even after a long day of slogging through wine mania, the UVA classes offered both freshness and exploration. More students were signing up every semester and they all had heard that here was something special. Winemakers making guest appearances, bringing barrel samples and wines from their private libraries, and conducting oak barrel blending seminars, got everyone even more excited.

Fortunately, the wine world was shifting out of its all chardonnay phase and into new wines made in the New World. Bringing in some of Oregon's finest pinot noirs to class was like being a happy pig rooting for truffles. After my years of roaming the Willamette Valley, I could sniff out an outstanding Oregon Pinot from a considerable distance. Suddenly, we became awash in them: Archery Summit, Domaine Serene, Ken Wright, Patricia Green and Panther Creek. They were delicious, and class was delirious.

Around that same time, California wineries were reverting to French-vineyard practices and winemaking styles. People were tiring of the big, fat, overblown wines and began to take a serious interest in wines emphasizing acidity and balance instead of raw power. Robert Mondavi's wines became the best to study because of their constant evolution through all of these styles.

Somewhere amidst all of the raving over chardonnay, a less popular white began to gain ground- sauvignon blanc. Tagging along in chardonnays shadow, it can't throw a football 40 yards, or turn as many heads, but sauvignon blanc was at long last becoming a hot grape. Sauvignon blanc had just entered into outer space, but without a space program.

Vineyard consultant Dr. Richard Smart (vine guru, not wine guru) came up with trellising systems that reinvented the flavors of grapes. His most revolutionary work at the time wound up with our old friend sauvignon blanc. You don't even have a definition of crispness until you taste these wines. Under his tutilage in New Zealand, the sauvignon blanc grapes burst forward resembling a ripe but highly charged grapefruit, gooseberry and kiwi combo. This region had been peeking through the window, now it was crashing the party.

Shortly after the New Zealand intro all hell broke loose. Every region and producer had a new grape to proclaim, giving every wine class teacher one more new grape to talk about. If the producer didn't have a new grape, he just put a twist on the old one to let the world know that it was there. Here are several examples.

Albarino: a northern Spanish white grape whose wine tastes of violets and peaches. You need to say "fresh and refreshing" as well as "don't age this one- it's a little like keeping roses in a vase too long. "

Fiano: an ancient white grape enjoyed by the Greeks and Romans that is making a comeback with the help of modern winemaking techniques. Heavy flowers and spice abound. Like albarino on steriods.

Arneis: it was nowhere, now it is everywhere. This white gem of a grape used to disappear into vats of tannic Barolo to soften the local red nebbiolo grape. Now, arneis is performing on its own in vineyards from California to Oregon. Nutty and powerful, with a distinctive flavor.

Gruner Veltliner: Austria (no, not Australia) came roaring back from obscurity and brought back with them their favirite white grape. This one has a distinct crisp flavor, different from unoaked chardonnay and from sauvignon blanc.

Petit Mansang: we're really talking obscure here, but growers are taking a whirl with this white grape fron a little known region of France called the Jurancon. To my tender buds it tastes like the white table grape juice that you buy at the grocery store. It is alarmingly aromatic, and the are people who love it. So there.

Through all the trends, I find teaching classes like being on a small boat in the middle of the ocean. Just when you start to get cozy with a grape variety, or a place, or a vintage, up blows a new wine and everything changes. In addition, the places that you take for granted suddenly capture the spotlight. Italy, wallowing and asleep producing its billion or so gallons of wine during the 70's and 80's, erupted in the 90's to become progressive and downright thrilling. Where DID pinot grigio come from? It has turned into its own Carnival Cruise of grapes, and now the entire planet is planting it as well.

Italy was paraded around as the prom queen for a decade or so. Winemakers, importers and distributors came through class to show her off. Even the old standby chianti's regular, classico and reserva became reborn into something wonderful. They metamorphosed themselves into something more than a wine to just splash down pasta.

At the same time France was slipping. She was once the wine class powerhouse, the whole reason that the rest of the planet even had the idea of planting grapes. France had suddenly turned into your older next door neighbor who brought you her famous macaroon cookies. You couldn't bear to look at that out of date snack. In the 90's I could introduce a few Macons into class along with some exciting wines from the Languedoc, but you knew that she just wasn't in the lead any more.

During this same period I sat next to an Australian winemaker for two days while we judged a competition. His comments were at the heart of the new overwhelming success of Australian wine. The place where the grapes came from wasn't on his front burner, the technique of how to transform them into supple, enjoyable wine was. Each time we tasted a wine, the wheels were going around in his mind thinking of ways to make it more drinkable. Every time I sit a have a glass of their fabulously successful shiraz I am reminded of that conversation.

What's next? Of course there is Spain bolting out of no where with those stylish and fruity reds for not a whole lot of money. There are a handful of whites, but the reds still rule. Could it be Austria? Those snappy gruner veltliners may become the next sauvignon blanc. What about those dry table wines from Portugal? And France has been busy reinventing itself through the rediscovery of enough little, obscure wine regions to last most searchers a lifetime. Or maybe a lone winemaker in a forgotten place will make the next big splash.

The Charts

Chardonnay Chart: Chardonnay and how it works:
Light To No Oak: Flavors of green apple, melon, and crispness. Prices run $10.00 and under. They come from: Southern France, the Languedoc, Loire Valley, the Rhone Italy (Veneto and Fruili), Chile, Argentina and California

Flavor Of Place: France: Flavors of slate, melon, citrus, earth. Little in the way of oak. Region and town and vineyard have their own distinct flavors. Places: Chablis, Bourgogne, Macon, Macon with town name (Vire, Clesse, etc), Pouilly Fuisse. Wines with oak: Meursault, Meursault Premier Cru, Puligny Montrachet, Puligny Montrachet Premier Cru, Chassagne Montrachet, Chassagne Montrachet Premier Cru.

Flavors Of Chardonnay With Oak: Lightly baked apple, lightly cooked pear, buttered toast.
California, Chile, Argentina, Oregon, Washington. A wine that says "barrel fermented" or "reserve" on the label. Price is a good indicator of oak aging,

because of the expense of oak barrels. Under $10.00 for a bottle of chardonnay means no or limited oak. $15.00-20.00 is medium and over $20.00 whatever the winemaker desires. The words "unwooded", now appearing on some bottles mean no oak regardless of price.

Sauvignon Blanc and how it Works:
Usually no oak, fresh, fruity, melon taste with slight herb taste. Dry and mellow: Chile, Argentina, Italy, France (Sancerre, Pouilly Fume, Languedoc- labeled as sauvignon blanc).
The French sauvigon blancs from town names are flinty, dry, assrtive and chalky.
California: called either sauvignon blanc or fume blanc. Can be herbatious, grassy, sophistated or have the flavor of oak.

Australia: similar to California. They can have bold and aggressive flavors due to the extreme ripeness of the grapes. Alcohol can be quite high.

New Zealand: kiwi fruit flavor with grapefruit intensity. Cutting edge, adds gooseberry and bitter Chinese melon to all the rest.

An Unbelievable Sauvignon Blanc Class:
The Robert Mondavi Winery has for decades pioneered styles of sauvignon blanc in California. You set up his tasting fron left to right (1-5).

1. Woodbridge Sauvignon Blanc, California: Light, simple fruit with soft sauvignon blanc flavor and character.

2. Robert Mondavi Private Selection Sauvignon Blanc, Coastal region. More complex, more flavor, no oak. It has that good Coastal light nelon acidity.

3. Robert Mondavi Fume Blanc, Napa Valley. Very lean and European in its tightly knit citrus flavors. Mirrors a Loire Valley Sancerre. In concept, it has passed out of California and into Europe.

4. Robert Mondavi Sauvignon Blanc Reserve, Napa. This wines moves us right back to California with its oak and powerful flavor.

5. Robert Mondavi "I" Block Sauvignon Blanc, Napa. This 75 year old sauvignon blanc vineyard is quintessential ancient Europe. A completely unique wine stretching the fruit flavor to tensile wire strength. It should be drunk while sitting on your moat.

One grape, one winery, five different interpretations. Which foods? 1. Guacamole. 2. Chicken, pasta and pesto. 3. Oysters. 4. Halibut. 5. Lobster.

The most important thing that I have discovered in teaching wine classes is that of creating strong contrasts in the wines that you taste. Small nuances work well when judging competitions, but for classes the lasting impression comes with contrast.

Reds: Three wines with a different pedicree and a different purpose:

Beaujolais- The fruity red from France. This is softness and light ness.

Zinfandel- California's own grape. Not too tannic but it usually has as much alcohol as fruit.

The Big Blend:
Cabernet Sauvignon- Full bodied wine, loaded with blackberry and cassis
Flavors
Merlot- Pure fruit at its most exhiliterating.
Cabernet Franc- An herby version of its cabernet sauvignon cousin.
Bordeaux- The great French red that invented the blending of all these grapes.
Line the four up and taste and blend to see how it is done.

Where does the grape come from:
Pinot Noir- One of each from Oragon, California, Burgundy and a sleeper like Argentina. Throw in New Zealand, too.

Where does the grape come from Part deux:
Syrah from California
Shiraz from Australia
Syrah from France that goes by the name of Cote Rotie

Petite Syrah from California. It isn't even the same grape.

The most amazing thing about teaching a wine class is that the material is in constant change, and all you have to do is to catch up to it. This won't be slowing down any time soon due to the wonders of DNA testing and the limitless source of grapes to test on. One day you wake up and your favorite grape suddenly has a new name and is from the wrong side of the tracks. The good news is that there are a whole lot of classes awaiting you to explain it. Teacher with a Glass is clearly about where you and your students are going on that journey.

Food and Wine

Since Catherine di Medici made the trek from Italy to France to marry the French dauphin and change her faith from Italian to French cuisine, someone has dutifully recorded every great meal in France. French food and wine ruled America for years, but in her homeland, France's mythical meals were more a form of gospel than nourishment.

As a rookie wine buyer standing at the bar of the French Club in San Francisco, I had the absolute lack of good taste to ask for a glass of Bordeaux before dinner. My French host gasped that my selection was out of the proper order, and would constitute a tremendous faux pas. I went home and immediately memorized the proper order of all French food and wine.

But after a few years of French food and wine, I was suddenly struck by what was going on: the French are stuck. Every meal —with the exception of their puny breakfast —is the equivalent of our Thanksgiving. Every meal is a meal where each dish is proscribed by mandate, ritual and culture. I wrote a little comparison chart on my breakfast napkin; a little revelation at my kitchen table.

Thanksgiving	French Meal	Wine
Oyster dressing	White fish and lobster sauce	White burgundy
Turkey	Rack of Lamb	Bordeaux
Cranberry Chutney	Salad	No wine
Pumpkin pie	Cheese course	Red burgundy
Pecan pie	Dessert	Sauternes

On the American side of the ledger, we can and will buy just about any wine for these courses. Once I formalized this comparison —namely by writing it on a "real" piece of paper —I realized that we Americans will suck up Aunt Mary's Genuine Giblet Gravy once a year, but to endure such formal, rigid rules as those of the French with any constancy is out of the question.

The last great event in the global ascendancy of French cuisine (and its accompanied wines) occurred during the mid-1980s. America was still enslaved to France's every dictate, as her local representative Julia Child reined supreme. In France, the most famous of all three-star Michelin chefs was due to receive his nation's highest award: The Legion of Honor (usually astronauts and entertainers receive this type of award in America).

To kick off the event, the chef showed up with a bevy of his colleagues and prepared a meal for the president of France (while all the news cameras were recording and disseminating the glory of the scene, of course). And what a glorious day it was, with the President munching away while Legion of Honor award winner Paul Bocuse stood by, puffed up in his chefs' whites and tri-color ribbon and medal while his minions frantically whisked, grilled and sautéed food. At the same time, sinister forces were at work in America. These forces had also figured out the uniformity of French cuisine, and they were going to do something about it.

These guerillas, dressed in black pajamas, conical straw hats and rubber-tire sandals, were David Rosengarten and Joshua Wesson. They were wine maniacs, food and wine writers, and soon-to-be gurus. Their underground tunnels and office complex was located in New York City. A friend slipped me a copy of their bi-monthly journal on food and wine and I was an instant convert. All I had to do was locate a pair of those cool rubber-tire sandals. Their journal questioned and probed every existing credo regarding food and wine. I was struck with the fork and corkscrew stigmata.

Their theory, as set forth in their newsletter, is that slavishly following the prevailing rules of food and wine "will kill you every time." Abandon the rules and follow your tastebuds. Try every food and wine combination you can; keep the good ones and discard the rest.

I immediately offered a rendering of their work in my wine classes at the University of Virginia. In the late 1980s, this stuff was culinary liberation. The students were knocked over. Everywhere my compadres and I went, we compared a flock of wines with another group of improbable foods and were rewarded with flavors we never dreamed existed. I wrote the guerillas a letter; one of those "I have been to the mountain top, and there you guys were with your conical straw hats, rubber-tire sandals and black pajamas noshing on some Vermont chevre and having a nice little Washington State sauvignon blanc." Their ideas were miraculous: Tuna steaks with pinot noir, or a thick, grilled ribeye with an oakey chardonnay. This was the New World.

Surprisingly, I got a letter back. They were pretty floored that someone actually turned their stuff into a class. Enclosed was their hot-off-the-press, just-published book Red Wine With Fish —The New Art of Matching Wine with Food. Whenever anyone says wine is snobbish, I turn to the autographed fly leaf and read the immortal words of author Josh Wesson, "To Layne: Don't let the paper bag touch your lips." I never have. Book in hand, I jaunted out to discover a new world of wine-food pairing in America. I went on a search for good matches, great matches, and even the learning experience that was to be had from bad matches. Americans finally had the opportunity to tune out our preconceived notions and use our minds to figure out what wines and foods worked.

My first sight of the erudite Joshua Wesson was on the podium. He was performing his wine class like Robin Williams, tearing up the audience with his shtick. The wine and food guru was awe-inspiring. From that moment on, I vowed to perfect this three at once form without notes: freewheeling, pacing and creating - turning the wine class into an art form. This would, of course, entail trying a different meal every night with a completely different wine, tasting things that hadn't been tasted together before (except, of course, for Thanksgiving).

We'll start at the beginning with my all-time favorite experiment: sushi. Line up all your favorite types: tuna, shrimp, octopus, salmon, squid, clam, abalone, and don't forget the eel whatever you do. Then line up glasses of the wines that best go with this array of fresh fish, wasabi and soy sauce. The best choices tend to be fruity and highly acidic (all the better to cut through that soy sauce and wasabi —not to mention the eel).

Vouvray: Loire Valley chenin blanc with plenty of crisp acidity; ranges from dry to fairly sweet. It is not terribly in fashion nowadays, and so its price-quality ratio is really in line.

German riesling, Mosel Valley Kabinett: The kabinett level of sweetness isn't all that sweet, but the combo of peaches and slate flavors are a knockout with the sushi.

Sauvignon blanc from New Zealand: You may love the kiwi and gooseberry one-two punch as it just slices through the fish (and everything else for that matter).

White burgundy: From Macon to le Montrachet will do, and so will everything in between. Some of the more serious white burgundies have too much oak, which will blow out the delicate flavors of the fish.

California or Spanish sparkling wine: Bubbles and sushi, what a treat.

Champagne: After trying tons of compatible and not-so-compatible wines, this is the one. It cuts through the soy, wasabi, and even the broiled eel with ease. It leaves your palate and you completely transformed. The other wines compliment the food but the refreshment of champagne's prickly acidity is the food and wine equivalent of a great day off.

My next quest to discover pairings that may or may not follow the rules involved the use of herbs. Take a chicken. By itself, it is pretty dreary stuff. But, when prepared with herbs it takes on a new life. Frankly, this is why people have herb gardens. Nothing tastes better than the stuff that has just been pulled from the ground.

Basil: A young fruity Chianti or Dolcetto. Chianti is living proof that some classics can not be improved upon. Which came first, the basil or the sangiovese grape? We probably will never know.

Dill: Pinot grigio or a crisp, acidic, sauvignon blanc. Bag the chicken and throw the dill on top of salmon for the best flavors.

Ginger: The real lost soul of wine and food is the gewürztraminer grape. Winemakers have finally decided that the over-the-top sweet mango flavors in gewürztraminer had to go away. Now, we can experiment with gewürztraminer in a variety of styles and regions from Washington state to Alsace to California to Northern Italy.

Mint: This is why local wine merchants still exist. They can guide you to a minty cabernet sauvignon or cabernet franc. A flavor combo to seek out.

Garlic: This "herb" should be a food group. Look for the "against the grain red." In our fruit-powered wine world, there are always a few "deliberate peasant" wines lurking around, wines that taste of the soil the grapes were grown in. France is still the main repository for these things. A nice old-fashioned Rhone or Chateauneuf, a Cahors, and any Bordeaux that hasn't been completely corrupted by modern civilization will all do the trick.

Mustard: Dishes get coated in mustard, and now what? A high acid riesling will cut through all manner and variety of mustard coatings. Plain out of the gourmet jar, it is usually a wine assassin.

Oregano: This herb was made for the world of Italian red wines. Barbara, dolcetto, montepulciano (both the cheap and the expensive ones) are all created to serve oregano.

Pepper: With its intense flavor, pepper really is a food group unto itself. Its intensity needs a counterbalance, and you can usually find that in a cabernet sauvignon or a particularly intense malbec. Although shiraz does have a pepper flavor, many are too fruity to stand up to real fresh-cracked pepper.

The great phenomenon of the 1990s was that every winery with an adventuresome soul and a budget hired or created its own wine-and-food expert. Theories flew wildly, and previously unknown combinations became the order of the day. Some stuck. Some didn't. Some never had a chance. California wineries have always been on top of change. They gleefully studied the new, and made it a part of their lives.

The difference between the old school, knee-jerk, follows the rules, food and wine pairing and "the boys' " theories of testing everything is that the modern system requires constant tuning. Not to mention keeping track of all the notes about what works and what doesn't. This kind of commitment resembles more the effort put into taking up a sport than in just fixing dinner. Tasting lots of wines comes with wine mania, and incorporating the findings comes with those strong collectors' mentality in having to catalog, jot down, and otherwise chase after that never-before-seen food and wine combo. This is Nirvana with a fork and corkscrew.

From time to time, I return to my copy of the guerillas' book, as it is still the most adventurous thinking ever on wine and food. One night, I decided to reenact a recipe for truffles and grits. The theory here is that the truffles (the very expensive fungus, not the chocolates) will be heightened by the nondescript flavor of the grits. An older, earthy Burgundy or Bordeaux, from an off vintage, will enhance the truffles' earthiness. A friend and I sat blissfully eating and drinking in the cloud of a dish that transformed the room and us into the culinary version of an ancient European wine cellar. This was what I call wildly original work.

There was a knock on the door and several friends came bursting in. "What are you eating? How is that wine?" I pulled up a couple of plates, got out a few glasses and feebly attempted to explain the genius of the food and wine pairing. It was a costly dish, and I had to trade an expensive wine to get the appropriately old and funky subject residing in our glasses. My friends shook their heads, opened the 'fridge and sucked down some chardonnay with a hunk of Monterey Jack. The spell was broken, and I haven't done that mystical pairing since. Great food and wine pairing has as much to with the moment as it does anything else.

So, the next time you go for a mango-encrusted sole with a chilled bottle of Beaujolais, or a hunk of salmon with pinot noir, or decide instead to have a rare fillet with a well-oaked chardonnay, remember "the boys." They had a large part in making all of this happen.

Finding Great Wine Dinners

You are constantly volunteering to do stuff in wine mania. The vintners, or winemakers dinner being the absolute prime example. When chefs and wine maniacs in America began to embrace the notion that they could experiment with vastly different foods and wines, that collaboration is continuously being enacted in restaurants of wildly diversified styles and places. The winemaker dinner was born and emerged fully formed. I have been a mostly eager participitant, doing several hundred over the years. Some have been glorious. Some absolutely atrocious. The wine maniac provides the commentary on the wines at each course. The chef worries endlessly in the kitchen, and then comes out to take his bows at the conclusion of the evening.

The idea is actually very simple. You create half a dozen courses, paired with interesting and unusual wines, both the chef and the wine person collaborate and are allowed to jointly run amok, expressing their individual creativity in the process. Depending on the abilities and imagination of the chef, and the palate of the wine person, these little artistic forays can be miraculous or disasterous. I have experienced my fair share of both. There are two terms used to depict this little culinary dance. A "winemakers dinner" features a winemaker showcasing his or her creations. Usually, at these, you will get a fair share of technical expertise. On the other hand, the "vintners dinner" is a non-winemaker, someone in wine mania who offers up a single winery, or a variety of wines depending on the event.

The driving forces behind these events can be several-fold. The restaurant wants to put themselves on the map, or make money on an off night, or do a reasonably priced special promotion for their customers, or simply take the opportunity to gouge their customers within an inch of their lives.

Likewise, the wine mania end of this little dance with delectables is entirely similar. To promote great wines, or to foist an absolute dog off on an unsuspecting public. At its finest, the vintner's dinner can be an introduction of new vintages, regions, styles, brands, or even grape varieties. When paired with imaginitave cuisine, witty discourse, and a less than backbreaking check a good time can be had by all.

The big question is, of course, how will you luck out and find the good ones. I have taken the liberty to classify then according to their quality for value. The lowest is naturally our old friend, "Would you pass that vinagrette to have with my Chateau Lafite, please?". This is the winemaker/vintner dinner where one or all parties want to squeeze every nickle out of you that they can and are hoping that you won't notice.

"The chumps night out" is a little higher on the ladder, but you have still only made it up to the third rung or so. The food is good, and the wine is good, but both are unimagnitive and overpriced. The greatest is our old friend the " wine maniacs". This is when the chef and wine person get in a zone and nothing gets between their creativity, not the greedy restaurant owner, nor the wine distributor wishing to foist lesser wines. It can be a reasonably priced dinner or costly and elaborate, as long as everyone is absolutely on.

The big question is "How the hell do you know which is which?" Our classic example occurred in a recent New York Times Dining Section. There it was- every vintners dinner in the world, and every question about whether or not it was going to be worth it. A little event's box of text two lines long announcing a Chilean Vintner wine dinner with nothing more than a price and a phone number. The price-$150.00 per person. Now, whatever you do never jump to conclusions. Make a list of questions to ask when you phone. This may be the absolute worst chumps night out or the greatest wine maniacs evening. Check it out. Give them a call. The first question is always, "Does this little event include tax and gratuity?" Your next question is, what's for dinner? Let's say that it runs something like this, my fictional

rendering mostly based on fact.

Hors d' oeuvre

Porotos Granados   Sauvignon blanc

A dish of beans, squash and corn

Appetizer

Oysters with breadcrumbs and cheese   Chardonnay

Soup

Gooseneck barnacle   #2 Chardonnay

Salad   (No wine)

Entree

Chancho a la Chilena   Cabernet Sauvignon

A pork casserole and vegetables

Dessert

Now, after you have the menu in hand, you need to obtain a list of the

prospective wines and the name of the evening's speaker. If they are a

national figure, the wine publications should have a mention of who they are. If they are a local person, simply call around to restaurants and shops to find out the level of talent that went into prying your money from you.

The most important thing about the wines is that they must live in the realm of the bucks that you are putting out. Get the list of what they are pairing with the menu and call your local wine merchant to get the retails on each. It goes like this for a $150.00 per person dinner: "Would you pass that vinaigrette to have with my Chateau Lafite, please?", together with a large helping of "Chumps Night Out", all rolled into one deliciously, dangerously overpriced dinner. Remember, there are lots of price levels within wineries, and unless you check the wines out you can be had.

One possible scenario: Concha Y Toro "Sunrise" Sauvignon Blanc, followed by Los Vascos Chardonnay and our #2 chardonnay from Casa Lapostelle and followed by the Cabernet Sauvignon by Errazuriz.

These are all good quality wines but they have one tiny flaw, they retail at between $10.00 to $12.00 a bottle. This is good work for your average Tuesday night, but won't cut it when you shell out $150.00, and your expectations are for great, unusual wine and food.

Here is the wine maniac's ultimate vintner's dinner for $150.00. Do a reserve Sauvignon Blanc by Casa Lapostelle. It is around $20.00 retail and is sensational. The chardonnay showdown would put both side by side through two courses: the top of the line "Don Melchor Chardonnay by Concha Y Toro. Very different wines from the Concha budget stuff that you see piled high in the clubs. The second wine comes from the folks who are best known for their cabernet in a fuzzy burlap sack. Their Chardonnay "wild ferment" by Vina Errazuriz is both sensational and offers up as a completely different style to the Concha Y Toro. Great stuff for wine dinners. Quality and contrast makes for a great evening. There has to be the freedom to choose wines that take the meal from a level of the merely interesting to a level of sheer fascination.

Everything should lead up to the wines for the entree, I usually like to pair two, and offer a striking difference to get the juices flowing and create conversation among the diners. It also makes for a lively presentation when you talk about both the wines and dishes. The Casa Lapostelle "Cuvee Alexander" Cabernet Sauvignon, aged in French oak is sophisticated and elegant. It settles you right in. You want to pair it with Domus Aurea, a wild untamed cabernet sauvignon, one of Chile's most uncompromising pieces of work. I would use the label by Chilean artist Benjamin Lira, a spikey haired profile of an anonymous South American Indian. Look before you aimlessly spend your money, the vintners dinner can be either a dazzling showcase or a money pit. It is your choice.

The greatest vintner's dinners are those events that are not engineered to make a ton of money for the restaurant on a Monday night, nor to enhance the wine distributor by moving his expensive, overpriced dog de jour wines that he mistakenly got overloaded on. The greatest ones that I have ever done are what you can say are organic they just appear naturally. The best example was assisting an old friend in wine mania. Kurt was Swiss trained, ramrod tall, and an impeccable European professional with tightly cropped grey hair, razor pressed attire and an ever present mineature Swiss flag on his jacket lapel. The phone call from out of the blue. He needed some help.

I hadn't seen him in years. He was the Food and Beverage Director for a giant hotel chain when I was with the Gigantic Wine Distributor. That was the last time we had the pleasure of being in wine mania together. He was now the F&B at THE local country club. As I drove up to the grand entrance, the place resembled The Parthanon on serious steriods, complete with all of the trappings of pretentious Early Classical Revival, the two story Corinthian columns a full four stories tall; this should be a cake, not a building. He had a great gig, all golf and lounging in the sun except for one small problem. Their restaurant business was all going to the golf and burger grill, and not to their Louis 16th dining room, as was planned.

Friendship is the real fuel of wine mania, and this guy had proven over the years to be a close friend. We had done a series of excellent wine lists together. I would do a couple of guest gigs for him in the Louis Palace, and only hoped that his chef could do more than a burger and fries for the golf set. We sat down to taste some of his dishes and check out his work. Here was a prodigious talent trapped behind the steam table making sure that the condiments were continually filled. He was not only up to the task but chuckled out loud as he said, "I relish it". We wound up doing about a dozen of these little gems, filling up the Louie Room with admiring and paying fans. The best publicity is always word of mouth. We trotted through the entire vintner's dinner repetoire including Basque, Thai, California, Provence and Tuscany.

The thing about vintners dinners is that they can be good, they can be exceptional, and occasionally they can be magic. There were three in the series that entered into the realm of pure magic. Chef had been bitching that he wanted to do pizza. Not ordinary, everyday pizza but cool pizza, pizza that made up for all those months messing with burgers and condiments. My idea was that the members, all patrician blue bloods should make the dough themselves. This idea was promptly shot down. The pizza evening took everyone by storm. Six courses, each of your own tiny pizza, accomanied with a different wine. The Four cheeses paired with pinot grigio. White pizza with roasted peppers, bacon and feta cheese accompanied by a glass of Verdicchio. Shrimp and crab with basil and tomatoes and a glass of Vernaccia. Winter vegetable with ricotta and mozzarella and a glass of Chianti Classico. Duck pizza with "lotsa veggies" and a glass of fine Dolcetto. Last was a cheese steak pizza with shaved beef and rooasted peppers and a glass of Chianti Classico Reserva. This was the first, and only, pizza night ever in the Louis 16th digs. It was completely out of the realm of both place and the blue bloods in the place. It was magic. The wines and foods should offer up the unexpected and then follow like a short, exciting journey throughout the entire evening. After we took our bows, this became the toughest to get reservation in town.

Lobster, that most amazing of all luxury foods makes for exciting vintner dinners, especially when you can move it from course to course, and wine to wine in exciting ways. It pairs well with all but the oakiest chardonnays. It amplifies the wines like a succulent stereo system, expanding both qualities and nuances you never dreamed of. Our Hors d'ouevres was none other than the old New England staple, the lobster roll, which I opened with a Spanish sparkler, a high quality cava. The cava offers up pure refreshment and gets you geared up for the ride. The appetizer, a potato, corn and lobster cake with a new wave Portuguese white albarino, a wine that can expand with amplification and change its multi faceter flavors. The zinger is the Jasper's New England Lobster Chowder, and the intro of a red wine- Thierry Mortet Bourgogne Rouge. Tomato base and lobster combined with pinot noir is fantastic, unexpected and moves the red the same way the lobster moves the white wine. You can't stop thinking about the lobster.... and the wine. The entree is a classic, Lobster thermidor with sugar snap peas and white truffle mashed potatoes. You can't stint on the budget here. This is the big one. Puligny Montrachet "Cuvee Nicole" Louis Carillon. White Burgundy brings this steel wire quality of flavor out of the chardonnay grape. It is lemony with the flavor of raw limestone, transferred from the vineyard where the grape is grown. It takes the luxurious oppulence of the flavor of lobster and bends and shapes it, changing the flavor and making it infinitely more complex. To my way of thinking, the lobster vintner dinner is one that the devotee of the entire genre always needs to experience.

Our wine masterpiece occurred when a wine importer called me at the store and announced that he had procured an unusual set of Champagne bottlings. I promptly phoned Kurt and chef and we put together a dinner. "Champagne, Champagne" was built around the fact that Champagne is usually a blend of three grapes: pinot noir, pinot meunier and chardonnay, all put together to form a final blend. Roger Pouillon, an exceptional producer, had put together a bottle of each grape variety and done up a blend of all three, a third of each wine in a larger bottle, and offered them as a set. There it was- be your own Champagne blender night.

The menu was different in style from pizza night where the food was king. Tonight Champagne was the king. Chef and wine mania at their harmonious best. The first Champagne was the pinot noir paired with the typically expected buckwheat blinis with caviar. The next Champagne was the pinot meunier with honeydew wrapped in Parma ham. We had an extra glass so that you could blend the two together to experience the how the Champagne master works with the lightness of the chardonnay and the delectability of the rarely tasted meunier. Salad and soup were Champagne enhancing creations, chilled potato and a pecan, scallion and green apple salad with the chardonnay Champagne. The main course was sea scallops, braised leaks, cream and fresh herbs alongside the winemaker's blend of all three grapes. We had so many Champagne flutes littering the tables we could barely reach our forks. At the end of the evening we knew exactly what a Champagne maker goes through to create magic in that bottle. The collection was never offered again.

Chef left to ski, hangout and occasionally cook in Colorado. Kurt left for a country club out of state. The new management requested that I do a return engagement of our old favorites with the new chef called "The Best of the Best". It was, of course, as we all knew it would be- the worst of the worst. You can turn in the most captivating performance, describing breathlessly the glories on their plates and in their glasses, but if it isn't there, it just isn't there. That was the last time that I spied those halls with the pictures of the ancestors. I didn't even look back for a glance at the tall, imposing pillars. Food and wine events can be planned and rehearsed, but the great ones are very much a work of art. They appear on your fork, in your glass, in brilliant comments about the wines. You can research to get the best deal, and it is wise to do that, but the talent of both chef and vintner when it all reaches perfection is an evening of pure magic.

Cork Dorks, Scroogies and the Rest

Six hundred years ago an anonymous group of monkish pilgrims revolutionized wine. Their wine flagons were sealed with carefully handcut stoppers carved from the bark of the quercus suba tree. They had created the first known corks. Prior to their discovery wine drinking mankind was forced to drink oxidized at worst and tired at best as their local wines. Experiencing the flavors of completely dead wine was far from unusual.

Their leather or wooden flagons with their new found cork seal created the first of modern wine as we know it. And like modern wine it can be fresh, slightly mature, or matured beyond all flavor. Who knows, but perhaps it was one of those first monkish travelers who turned into and became the first cork dork. Succeeding generations have gladly followed his lead.

I blame restaurants for the propetuation of the species. The cork is removed from the bottle and placed in front of the startled diner and his equally intimitaded date/ spouse and all hell breaks loose. The diner picks it up, sniffs it and, at worst, takes a little bite, just to assure himself that he is doing the right thing. Lately, it is the woman at the head of the table who gets to endure the same form of exquisitite pseudo pleasure. What is to be gained or learned by being a certified card carrying cork dork? Nothing. The cork teaches nothing. It is either good or bad, and that is it. If it is good, then the wine follows and it too is good. If it is bad, then the wine reeks and is usuallt undrinkable and that is it. So much for eighteen generations of cork dorkdom.

Lately, the cork has fallen upon hard times. There is even a large, influencial, and highly vocal group that I call the " scroogies " whose aim is to eliminate the cork all together. The problem with corks originated a few years ago when consumers, wine writers and wineries began to notice an acrid, wet cardboard and damp basement smell coming from the glasses of their favorite wines. The worst part of all of this is that you can not judge the wine's condition from a look at the outside of the bottle. Also, it is when you pull the cork of that expensive bottle that you have been hoarding for that special event, that the wet basement smell waifs from cork to glass to your nose, announcing that your money might as well reside in that same basement.

There are lots of problems here. To start, the cork infestation has a long, unpronouncable name: 2,4,6, trichloranisol, that in itself is a problem, so the wine maniacs have just knocked it down to TCA to make everyone just that much more comfortable with that whiff of cardboard in their glass. The biggest, most daunting problem is just how many bad corks are out there? This is what makes wine mania so truly exciting. Some wineries insist that only 1-2% of their wines have contaminated corks, while others emphatically state that anything less than 10% is out of the question. No one is certain how many bad corks are in your future, whether the wine costs $5.00 or $505.00 a bottle. At least there is some form of democracy. The only good thing is that bottle you bought for your birthday can be exchanged when it is discovered to be corked. It is the occasion that has all the fun of a car having the air let out of its tires.

When you seriously look into the problem and look into the "who's to blame" part, it comes down to a simple problem of chlorene and mold as the culprits creating the dreaded TCA. Warm and damp environments are their playgrounds. The game works like this: cork factories are blamed by the wine growers for being nonchalent and sleasy while the factories, in turn, blame the myriad cork brokers for trying to make too fast a buck and turning their backs on quality control. The cork industry P.R. people blame the wineries for ordering and demanding too low a quality and price for their corks. Unfortunately no one in the cork manufacture and distribution chain seems to worry about you with your little birthday hat on and a glass of stinko wine in your hand that you just shelled out a cool $95.00 for. Tough.

The first wave of winery resentment appeared a few years ago in the form of little polyeurathane plastic corks replacing the real thing. The more descrete wineries offered them in brown or hues of tan with a touch of faux graining for real cork like effect. The wineries that were more statemant oriented introduced yellow, red, black, white and vibrant colors. You could not possibly mistake one of these for a real cork. They allied the fears of bad corks for awhile until the problems of too tight a fit (you couldn't possibly pull it out), or the fit was so loose that the polyeurethane just fell into the bottle with a little "plop". As long as you were going to drink that bottle tonight it would usually be OK, but the wineries and consumers both became as nervous as with the mouldy cork itself.

In the early 1990's one of America's largest wineries made a major switch. Sutter Home replaced the corks on their 1.5 liter bottles with screw caps. The sales meeting that I attended for this august occasion was one of handwringing and brow wiping. It was also hysterically funny. The austute winery sales management team refered to their new cork replacing caps as Stelvin Closures (after the name of the maker). They implored that under no circumstances were we ever to refer to them as " screw caps", and they were looking over their shoulders in a highly paranoid fashion. The irony was that the people who drank the stuff were probably thrilled that they didn't have to go out and buy a corkscrew, and could casually pour it into their prize jelly jars while watching NASCAR.

Less that a dozen years later the screwcap has undergone a complete metamorphosis. In wine mania there are usually signature moments, events of dynamic force that change everything. We all knew that the Sutter Home meeting was not one of them. The events that changed it all were the "death of the cork" dinner and the revolt of the scroogies. On October 2, 2002 there was an all black (costumes and food) memorial dinner to celebrate the death of the cork. It was a stylish celebration commemorating the cork's 500-year ride and its final demise. A small corpse like cork was paraded through Grand Central Station in New York and was eulogized by no less a personage than Jancis Robinson, a wine guru of much greatness and renown. This was maximum anti-cork firepower. A full frontal assault on the shortcomings and demise of the cork, complete with dinner (black food), speeches (also black), and a special eulogy by Jancis herself leading with "How we shall miss thy cylindrical barky majesty?". How shall we? All present felt that they wouldn't at all.

The ringmaster and head scroogie was none other than Randall Graham of the Bonny Doone Vineyard, announcing, as a continual thorn in the side of cork producers, that he was bottling a substantial amount of his wines in screw caps. Even though they were Stelvin Closures, the term was screw cap, loud and clear. Mr. Graham, a wine maniac of the highest order, is of course, a master of public relations, and did raise every bit as much a fuss a few years back when he experimented with polyeurathene. Alliances do change.

Let's face it. In spite of the barky bombast, and even Mr. Grahams change over to 80,000 cases of screw caps, this wasn't really enough to stem the tide away from 'ol barky himself. That drop from the proverable cork bucket did make considerable noise, what with the estemmed members of the wine press falling all over themselves to write that story (myself included). The word for the story was -delicious.

The real screw cap gusher occurred when Hogue Cellars out of Prosser, Washington decided to take the project on and convert some six million bottles annually. There was barely a whiff of publicity from the winery, but the effect of having such a gigantic and respected player in wine mania make the change was enormous indeed. While Mr. Graham was flailing about and pushing his barky little casket through Grand Central

Station, the folks from Hogue in their quiet and effective way were making a serious dent in the consciousness of the cork by offering a high quality wine that many had tried, and this time it would have a screw top.

Ironically, at the same time, screw caps began spilling in from New Zealand and Australia in a dramatic fashion. These were $10.00 to $20.00 bottles of wine, all from quality producers. No pretensions here, just unscrew it and go. This was not dramatic, even though we believed it so. What was dramatic was Plumpjack. Gordon Getty, nepotist and wine maniac par excellence, decided to stick a screw cap atop a $150.00 bottle of cabernet sauvignon, and just for thrills do a similar bottling with a cork. You decide. Of course, if you tasted from both bottles side by side, people would assume that either you were loaded with money, were completely out of it, or were really on to something. Being fortunate to have had both, at a birthday party no less, I decided that he really was on to something both in terms of publicity and quality in that pair of glasses. Plumpjack got all of wine mania talking.

The best-recorded case of spontaneous eruption against the cork in wine mania was the wine writers' revolt against the tainted cork, or old barkey as he has come to be known. Probably no one pulls more corks as a group than wine writers do. When they get off or on to something it is a form of collective uncosciousness. At the exact moment that the cork P.R. people were crooning and submitting their press releases that the future for the cork couldn't look brighter, the wine writers by 2003 had all the cork industry hype that they could stand. Their titles told it all. "Popping Corks: A Sound Bound for Oblivion", Frank Prial, N.Y. Times. "Uncorked: Beware, There is a Screwcap coming to a Restaurant near you" by me at Style Weekly. "Corked Off" by Ben Giliberti, Wash. Post. "Screw Tops: Get Used to Them" same at Wash. Post. All of these little gems in 2003 alone. Is there a pattern here? Yes, we are all very pissed off.

How did it come to this? Wine writers see and experience all of the propaganda- from wineries, cork producers, the public, and they open and taste thousands of bottles of wine a year. We are the microscope and litmus paper of our little subject. So don't piss us off with mindless press releases. You may be able occasionally to fool one of us but to try to do so continuously will be at your own peril. While some are gurus we are not serene Buddhas. 2003 was not a banner year for cork people. Their only good news was some disagreement among wine writers about the future and extent of the screw cap. But that was it, all else was pretty bleak for the cork people.

Ben Ghilaberti, wine columnist for the Washington Post is one who believes that screw caps are a good thing for moderate and lower priced wines but are reaching too high when it comes to the rarified heights of the $100.00 bottle. But, his remidy for the consumer having a corked bottle in a restaurant is pure draconian (and viewed by the restaurenteer with complete dread). His idea is to have the flawed bottle replaced with a sound one and having the customer not be charged for the second bottle. We could call this the penalty phase of dining out. The wholesaler will make good on the first; the restaurant will eat it on the second.

The replies to this historic piece of modest proposal-making ranged from the local restaurants clammoring with indignation that they would lose the sale from the second (and all that delicious 300% markup). They howled that they weren't the guilty parties, but were being penalized nonetheless.

Of course, the consumers were gleeful. This was sort of like winning the $50.00 plus lottery without putting out your buck. While the idea is a bit wild the cork producers have been passing the buck up and down the line without having to face anyones monetary recriminations. Maybe the restaurants could just work up a return coupon that they could mail off to the cork manufacturers with every bad bottle. That very interesting and clever idea of Mr. Ghilabertis may go away for awhile, but it will with time bubble up to surface again. Fascinating ideas like that just don't die.

It is one thing to encounter some corked wines in the routine of tasting a lot of wines for publication, but it is another during that rare lapse away from wine mania. When not doing all of this wine stuff I slip away into the passion of collecting modern art. Many of the artists don't even know what I do for a living. It beats the hell out of golf as you can hang it on the wall and observe it for years, and you can do your part to help promote a local artist. One of our local artist couples took us out to dinner not long ago as a little thank you for our support. We were happily into our fifth Thai dish and awaiting the arrival of our second bottle of wine. We were into a lively discussion on local painters when I reached down and tasted the wine. It was corked. Wet basement, nasty, knock-down, bad assed corked. My wife looked over with her look. She could smell my glass from where she sat. I decided to say nothing. A grandiose announcement would have killed our exciting evening. "It's bad?" "Why is it bad?" "Corked you say, what's that?" "Corked?" We drank less than a half glass apiece. The bottle slowly faded from sight, the glasses were replaced, and the wine was followed with one that was good. It was all painless and quiet, but I still didn't forget that corked bottle.

As all of this was occuring I gained the best insight ever on what a corked wine actually is. Wonderful, exciting wine is an enhancement to a fine meal and lively conversation. A corked wine, if you let it, can take over and kill the moment, the food and the evening. When you think of it, the modest proposal of that 2nd bottle for free is not that high a price. And sending the bill for your dinner to the cork producer isn't that high a price either. No other group in wine or restaurants take as blaise an attitude about the enjoyment of our lives.

The scroogies are howling, but hopefully they will put deep pressure on the cork manufacturers to clean up their act and provide 100% quality corks. As more wineries are testing the results of corks against screw cap in quality, the short-term results are in. Screw caps are holding their own. It will ultimately be the wineries that decide which way the battle goes. Wineries are naturally cautious although the scroogie wine writers are speaking with a big stick. Many super-premium wineries like Murphy Goode are bottling their 2nd label in screwcaps and are looking to see what will happen. It is this kind of experimentation that predicts the onslaught of the screw cap over the cork. A large shift to screw caps by a high volume and high quality brand like Beringer would give cork manufacturers both a humbling as well as the time to get their quality act together in time for a comeback. The scroogies will be the first to applaud.

Wine Books

Wine books capture the soul of the subject at its best. They give us the entire banquet, up to the port and plateful of walnuts. Every December a crop of new wine books comes off the press. They are the new sets of ideas about the subject, the new controversies, and equally important, the new stories that set everyone talking. Along with the wines themselves, books provide the lifeblood of wine mania. Sure, there is still the equivalent of a wine writer falling asleep and publishing a mish mash of tired old stuff that make us let out a loud, alarming yawn and a sigh. When they are good, they are really good. The following are among the most enthraling wine books I have ever found, the ones that both teach and fascinate for a wide variety of reasons. These are the ones that, to me, have made a difference between what you routinely find and what is truly unique and original. Not to say that there isn't other good work out there. There is. Here are some of my alltime favorites in wine mania, books that I have used for amusement, teaching and inspiration.

The first post modern wine book. We all woke up one morning, and there it was. Hugh Johnson's <u>The World Atlas of Wine</u>, Simon and

Schuster, 1971. After the pricemeal little wine travel guides of the period, this was an utterly different look at the subject. It just happened to coincide with the wine revolution of the 1970's and the emergence of new, exciting regions and flavors. You opened it up to a detailed panorama map that not only revealed the place for the first time, but also explained to you the quality heirarchy and why wines both taste and cost the way they do. This book is still relevant, and it's still in print. If you should be touring and poking around wineries that began in the 1970's you are certain to see an old, tattered, much used copy of this book in their back room. It's where their early inspiration came from. And it is probably one of the first references they turn to today.

A book that I have used more than any other in both teaching and travels is a small, obscure, out of print work by the British wine merchant/author Simon Loftus. Anatomy of the Wine Trade: <u>Abe's Sardines and other Stories</u>. An indespensible, hands on look at a British wine merchant at work. It is quirky, irreverant and a downright scathing portrait of the high and mighty in the Bordeaux trade. If you ever feel that their prices are way over the top, then pick up this book, for he points his sharp finger at the noses of the culprits. In his chapter o The Bordeaux Commodity Market he gleefully compares and contrasts the purchase of that fine

Bordeaux that we so admire with the purchase of a tin of sardines that you would aimlessly throw in your shopping cart. And he pulls it off.

His road trips co-incide with the generation of American wine buyers in the 1980's in Europe. There he is, in that little armadillo car, filled to the roof with clothes and wine samples. What he discovers along the way is a revolution in thinking and quality in a place with too many poor local traditions. He pulls apart Europe in front of our eyes, and he puts it back together again as well. Twenty years later, this book reads like it is fresh and new, and you can still carry it around in your little armadillo car.

This is living proof that you don't exactly have to like a book to put it on your list. It is Joy Sterling's A Cultivated Life: A Year in a California Vineyard, Villard Books, 1993. This condensed little nugget of moosh covers all aspects of grape growing, wine making and marketing (Joy's job) for Iron Horse (her nepotist family's winery). It covers important subjects such as where to get your rootstock and how to blend and bottle your sparkling wine. There are also little indespensible tips such as the placement of the table to seat 500 guests. This is not a typo; it is one table for 500 guests. Also, a favorite is the gala replanting of the wildflowers (and I thought they just grew.... wild) at $100.00 per pound for the seeds.

The only thing missing from all of the high toned chatter is a chapter entitled" Why they call it La La Land?" This chapter should acquaint all of those who live outside of California to the art of celebrity name-dropping. It will also introduce you to all of those famous names that you may or may not be familiar with- but should be. Everyone from Wolfgang Puck to The Dutchess of Mouchy pops up here, with hundreds of glitterati inbetween. There are better books on wine, but none better to use to study up for life on the red carpet, where each of those 500 people make it to that table, all at the same time. If you wish to plunk down the folks money on a trophy winery in a fashionable zip code in California, this book is required reading for it truly is the ultimate nepotist's handbook. Also, it will be a valuable guide when you and your accountant have your desperate little huddle sessions. Just go through it and add up all of those expenses. Remember, this was written during the heady glory days of the California economy. And don't forget the seed for the wildflowers.

We were all slurping on our small flavor merlots when suddenly one day it took us by complete surprize: the take over and utter domination by the syrah/ shiraz (whatever that was?) grape. The great guide through these changes is Remington Norman's <u>Rhone Renaissance: The Finest Rhone and Rhone Styles: Wines from France and the World</u>, Wine Appreciation Guild,

1996. Seems that the syrah grape has quite the reach, both in places grown and in names that it is referred by. In Europe, the place, and in Australia and California the grape, with syrah and shiraz interchangable. Now, if all of that doesn't require a book, then nothing does.

If you are looking for names and lists of wineries, there are books that list more of them. But, if you are looking for the real reasons that wines taste the way they do, then this is your best stop. He doesn't list all the producers of these grapes, but does go into an in depth look at the region where the grape is grown and an anylitical cellars eye view of how the winemaker is working his magic. He is wise to use the name Rhone Renaissance since lots more grapes are making an appearance to blend with syrah. Your one stop Rhone style wine book.

Coffee table, smoffeetable books, who wants them? How can one agree on a subject any more than this? The front cover always has some winemaker's trophy wife out in the vineyard, cluelessly raising aloft a bunch of trophy grapes- the most beautiful little cabernet sauvignon grapes in the world. So what? There is one book that defies the stereotype of all that surperflous crap. The Architecture of Wine by Dirk Meyhofer, Gingko Press, 2000. It should be subtitled 'And the drama of wine.' They only feature photos and text from twenty wineries (eight from Bordeaux and twelve from the Napa Valley), but they manage to squeeze every ounce of drama and emotion from every single façade, setting and architectural detail.

Fortunately, this is an architect's view of wine mania and those boring pieces of standard winemaking equipment are relegated to the back of the picture. There are fascinating modern additions to older buildings that make the viewer look hard and ponder. The architectural details from the chateau make you remember how long they have been palaces to transform the grape and delight us. The selection of Napa and their modern, art driven, one-step-ahead wineries gives the book its lift. Just as you get settled into the 18th century seraglio eccentric style of Chateau Cos d'Estournel, then a few pages later you are thrust into into the modern, artistic fantasyland of Napa's Clos Pegase. The best thing about this book is that you won't become tired of it. There is always something to appeal to both your eyes and your imagination. Yes, and you can even put it on your coffee table and people won't laugh.

Since wine books have the uncanny ability of always celebrating something, one of the finest examples of the genre is Paul Lukacs American Vintage: The Rise of American Wine, Houghton Mifflin, 2000. A real rags to riches story, and ironically it is all about American wine. The Europeans have always had the big crunch over us when it comes to quality wine. They have always ruled. Poor America. We enact prohibition, and then after prohibition the winemakers taste and evaluate the wines, only to find that the best of a sorry lot aren't the dry table wines but the ghastly sweet fortified ones. So, its port and muscatel that ruled for decades.

Then in the 1960's a few Californians hike over to Europe and proclaim that they should be able to make wines like that. They return to California with their work ethic strongly in tow, and a model in their minds for what they want to do. It is all Europe transported back to the states. This book is like a highly readable narrative saga of the march of American wine. Even though you know how it will end, you frequently forget and become concerned. It ends with Steven Spurrier in 1976 on the roof top garden of the Inter-Continental Hotel and those French judges proclaiming how "Tres complet" that blind tasted wine was. Yes, the very same wine that they thought was French but actually was from California. The day their rule ended. America, and much of the rest of the world, would be dominated by the flavor and power of the grape name and no longer bow to the ancient European rule of the town and place name on a label.

Fabulous Fizz by Alice King, Time Life Books, 1999 is as personal a journey as exists in the subject of wine. Just by picking this book up and glancing at it, there is a feeling that the author completely inhabits this small space. Usually, I question whether another wine book is necessary, or that it will fit in the already overcrowded wine book shelves. Not here. I bought it on first sight, shelves be damned.

Opening her book puts you in a mood right away. Pictures of corks, and fizzy bubbly glasses greet you like there is something to celebrate. Celebrate right now, it says. She covers her subject, not like a person who has studiously prepared, but like a person who is immersed in every possible nuance and could be found on a street corner proclaiming it to the world. She gives forth her own personal recommendations, complete with one sentence snappy quotes on each wine. The book is small in pages, loaded with pictures and always sends me to the fridge for a glass of Champagne when I am done reading. Now, that is an irresistable book.

You can't have a top wine books list without including Matt Kramer somewhere in the fray. There is a certain quirky quality to his work, like Indiana Jones and Che Guevara sitting together to write a book. The problem with his books is that he makes you work for it. No cozy 90 point scores here. No handful of brezzy wine tasting catchwords either. You have to go through line by line like a monk, remembering those important passages.

His <u>Making Sense of Burgundy</u>, Wm. Morrow, 1990 scares up the image of him and his gnomes crawling through those dusty provincal

Burgundian town halls rummaging through the ledgers of who owns what little sliver of which vineyard. No one has done it before, the ultimate in monkish work. Not in a humorous sense, because it does sound funny, but for the earnest lover of Burgundy to have a track on what things really are in a land where serious information ranges from difficult to impossible. It is not a closed society, they just don't pay a lot of attention to outsiders.

This book transports you into the heart and soul of a place like no other book on wine. He takes you through the minefields of poor quality vineyards and slapdash winemaking and delivers you straight into the chapter "The Notion of Terroir", the greatest single chapter on understanding how the flavors of European wine reveal themselves. This repudiates all that you have read, and much of what you have tasted about wine. The "varietal", chardonnay or pinot noir have no sway here, nor do the winemaker's ego or equipment. Burgundy at its best is the mystery of the flavor of the land. You think through how completely different they are from New World Wines. No intensity of super ripe fruit, the searing power of new oak barrels, the ego of the winemaker in every glass. This is the elegance and gentleness of the incomperable flavors of a unique place.

After the French Revolution the vineyards were sold and carved up from generation to generation. Unfortunately, for those of us raised on varietal grape names those vineyards are a mystery to us. Fortunately after Kramer and his cohorts' gigantic camp out in those town halls we can see who has the best morsels of which slivers of land. This remarkable book does several things exceedingly well. It converts those vineyards into a travelogue in your mouth. You then can pin point and look up what exactly any given grower makes. You tend to think of California trophy wines as miniscule, but they have nothing at all on Burgundy. You can still find wines made in less than fifty cases and not pay a fortune. The Che Guevara part of this book is that he goes after growers who use those coveted place names to rip us off. The little power to the people part. The Indiana Jones part of this book is the opening up of a treasure cave that we knew existed but had only seen in pictures. Now we can taste it for ourselves.

The last book in our little excursion is very opposite of the others. With Kramer you study with the presision of the scholar, lest you miss a single transforming thought. Our last book is not that: it is a pure read. You sit down with a bowl of casoulet and a bottle of red Bordeaux on the table, and you devour all at a single sitting. The book is Wine and War: The French, The Nazis and the Battle for France's Greatest Treasure by Don and Petie Kladstrup, Broadway Books, 2001. You already know several things about the book before you open it. Who won. Who lost. That the French hid a lot of their wines during the war, and that the Germans scrounged about during the countryside trying to find them.

This is a great read because it covers well the scurring French being chased and hounded by the hobnailed, jackbooted German troops. That is a small part. What really makes this book great is that it confirms the importance that wine has on European culture and it shows the human condition at its best, and at its worst. From its opening the authors are in charge of the stories, both humerous and sad. Wine is about stories. This isn't a backdrop but is the fabric that courses throughout. Also, the French consider their wine as both a symbol of their country and an economic and patriotic asset.

The Nazis did the quick invasion of France, with their trucks poised just behind the army to extract as much booty as possible. Two million bottles of Champagne were quickly swallowed up into a convoy of trucks. From the restaurants of Paris, to Loire Valley caves, to the vast chateau of Bordeaux, the wine riches of France provided a bounty beyond description. Field Marshall Herman Goering had already pin pointed his desired riches.

Each region of France carried with it stories and tragedies of the war. In Alsace, the Hugel family was used to war. Grandfather Emile changed nationalities four times in his life; such is the problem of being wedged between Germany and France. War was tough on the winegrowers, especially with tanks crossing through your vineyards.

The Champagne region was clobbered economically through pillage. When the Germans did buy, they set the prices and bought cheap. The growers quickly bottled the very worst stock they could find with special labels for the German army. The best wines of Champagne were hidden behind hastily constructed walls. The Germans appointed a Weinfuhrer to oversee the area, with the cat and mouse game beginning in earnest. Several Champagne producers were thrown into prison when their foisted off, less than adequate wines were tasted by a German who knew their stuff.

The other cat and mouse game was the growers letting the resistance hide food, weapons, and themselves in their caves. Now, apart from spending a few months in prison, the grower could be shot. Tensions grew, and the workers of Champagne did the unheard of- they went on strike. There were military tribunals, fines and the Weinfuhrer abruptly took charge of a major Champagne house. Things finally quieted down.

There were winegrowers that suffered terrible trials and tribulations. One of the Huet brothers from the Loire Valley landed on the Russian front, the other was captured and spent the war in a POW camp. Gaston was interred in a 4,000-prisoner camp suffering from malnutrition for several years. He discovered a glitch in camp rules and did receive packages of food from home. They could also receive wine. Gaston in great need of morale thought up the idea of having a festival among the prisoners to celebrate their culture. It would take 700 bottles to provide each POW with a glass of wine. From a one day event the idea spread into a month long fete with songs, skits, costumes and scenery. The planning became their most important means of survival. The event happened and each POW had his tiny glass of wine. "It was nothing special, and there was only a thimbleful, but it was glorious, and the best wine I ever drank" Huet had lost half his weight during his internment.

As the war was ending the Free French army was heading toward Hitler's lair at Berchtesgaden, his private wonderland in the alps. They were determined to take back their stolen treasures, the art, the jewels, and the world's finest wines. For Lieutenant de Nonencourt this trip was full circle. He watched helplessly as the Nazis pillaged his native Champagne and now he had the honor of leading the first troops into Hitler's lair. There were hundreds of thousands of cases of wine that had to be loaded down by stretchers as the ascent was steep. The Americans and French filled their canteens with great wines and toasted to the liberation. De Nonencourt drank the Champagne that he had helped to make, and that he had seen hauled away. Wine had never tasted better.

Shop 'Till You Drop

I have been from my earliest (legal) days an inveterate wine shop browser and shopper, and wound up becoming a buyer for a wide variety of stores. I discovered that you can classify wine shops in basically three forms: the mahagony showplace, the discheveled garage and the greeting card palace, comlpete with paper napkins and a bit of wine thrown in. Even though the three store types have different styles and personalities their appeal all boils down to several things. First, is there a decent ongoing selection to keep you interested and coming back? ? Second, are they trying to screw you with their prices? Third, and by far the most important, is there an in house guru to help guide you through the everchanging maze of wines?

The mahogany showplace may charge more just to pay the upkeep from their high priced furniture restorers. Always make a list of half a dozen brands that are not in supermarkets that these three stores would carry in common. You won't know which is the most reasonable until you compare all of them- looks can be decieving. If the mahogany palace does have higher prices, but also has a killer selection, and a wine guru, then just suck it up and support that restorer.

The discheveled garage is my alltime favorite wine shop. Boxes are strewn everywhere, and a very large, hairy dog is sprawled in the Champagne aisle. The proprietor is unkempt and has halitosis. These are the prime ingredients leading up to a great garage wine shop experience. The wines should be eccentric and eclectic, little known treasures that hail from places that few people know. There may be a guru present but the conversation about wine will take place while they are moving all those dusty boxes around. This is complete, no frills wine shopping and if you aren't afraid to get a bit dirty it can be rewarding.

Our last wine shop is the most difficult to figure out. The greeting card palace (with paper napkins) may have a deli in its midst so that you can enjoy a bite while observing all of the foof around you. All of the figurines and paper things are making a statement- buyer beware. This type of shop is usually located in a mall where the rent is high. Also, the paper stuff has a huge markup. Is this philosophy being passed on to the wine? Do your list of six drill and see how they stand in their prices. They should be using a standard margin for the everyday stock items and it won't take but a few minutes to tell. Check the card aisles for a guru, as you never know. The classic way that the greeting card shop can fake you out is by hanging all those millions of shelf talkers with inane wine descriptions all over every bottle in the store. They are computer printed and can be from wine writers that no one in the store has ever heard of. The biggest problem for you is to equate these little obnoxious tags with the staff's actual knowledge in the store. Ask if the store person has tasted these wines and agrees with what is written on the tags. I usually look for hand written tags, which means that at least someone in the store tastes the stuff and knows what they are doing. In store wine tastings are an effective form of getting some of your money, at least when they are pouring the wine. Don't pass them up, but don't let your life revolve around them either. Finding that guru in the store when the bottles aren't open is a better bet for the long run.

The ultimate test of any wineshop is that they aren's staffed exclusively by college students trying vainely to pretend that they are in wine mania. They are in mania, all right, but it isn't wine mania. Your best bet is to find a guru or gurus to steer you through the maze of complicated places, names and prices. This is clearly worth the extra couple of bucks.

A recent arrival in the world of wine stores is what is affectionately termed the category killer. These resemble conventional wine stores the same way that you and I resemble a tackle in the NFL. You tend to squint as your face greets the middle of his chest. " This dude is really big", you say to yourself. Upon entering a category killer you see how they got the name.

It is as if every wine shop in the world was stacked, packed and stood at attention several stories in height. You really need to be observant here. Make two lists- one for the usual brands that are commonly found and the other for their featured stuff, the wines that are piled highest in the store.

In this type of store you can go on a Kendall Jackson, Santa Marguerita, binge. All the national brands are way low in price. But that is not what you are here for, w hether you know it or not. Their plan is for you to go on a feeding frenzy with their brands, the ones they created especially for you. The ones they make their money on. Now comes your second list. Do a variety of comparisons with their labeled wines of Chianti, Alsace and Bordeaux. Also try that $15.00 bottle of California wine that you have never heard of. Trot them home and put them side by side with those that are similar in place and price from the discheveled garage guy. This is the only way to become a smart wine buyer and not just someone who throws stuff in a shopping cart.

If the category killer has a guru, and some of them do, it is smart to listen to their recommendations. You know going in that you will be handed their own labels, but at least if the guru is honest and straightforward you will be getting the best value and most interesting stuff. Still, it's not a bad idea to compare as every buyer has both their own palate and contacts. The last thing that you want a category killer to do is to kill your wallet, and not excite you taste buds.

While we have our shopping cart at the ready, let's go to the grocery store. Grocery stores are as vast in style and selection as any form of shopping experience. So with that in mind, we'll look at several types. The discount, no frills grocery store also has a discount, no frills wine department. You really need to carry your short list of brands with you here. Only the national stuff will do, as you won't find any others in the discount grocery chain. While your selection is decidly slim and a guru won't be in sight (unless the guy in the produce department just happens to be taking a wine class) you can do well here as long as you stick with the sale wines or know which have he best prices.

The mega grocery store, or super store as it is called, is trying to prop itself up as the wine store of the future. They stock thousands of wines, feature a hundred or so displays, have a wine guru in residence, and in spite of all that something is still missing. When you peruse carefully (leave your list at home today) it looks like all of those labels could have been made by about six wineries, so eager are they to imitate the wine fad of the moment. It is a fast food display all done up as a super selection.

In this type of store, in this corporately constructed wine world, shelf tags are the key. They can sometimes represent fabulous savings. Depending on what their competition is doing, you can sometimes find a solid known quality at near or below cost. If you are lucky and the wine steward/guru is about, you could get the 'A' tour of the shelf tag maze of interesting wines and their best values. It is still smart to carry your list because even the mega/super store may have a week when the display wines all taste and look alike and the deals are uninteresting. This is the time you want to throw yourself on the mercy of the discheveled man and his hairy dog, and maybe help him move a few of those dusty boxes.

As more wineries are gobbled up by corporate wine mania giants there is a creeping similarity in what you see. This is especially true when the mega grocery stores get carried away in the fray. Have you seen more than one fuzzy koala bear, cute little penguin, multi colored kangaroo or other form of marsupial on a wine label lately? Likewise California has their own little thing going on as well. The operative word here is oak. Oak House, oak boat, oak rock, oak bench, and the irony is that none of the wine inside these labels of oak frenzy (usually chardonnay and merlot) has seen more than the barest smidgen of oak —ever. The only good thing is that these wines are both reasonable in cost and aren't disgusting for the paltry sum they are charging. There won't be any surprizes here. This is your entry into the homoginized world where your choices are few but they are all deals. Just make sure that your taste buds inform you that you aren't buying the same wine under five different labels.

The big box stores or wholesale clubs are both the easiest and most disconcerting places to shop for wine. The chances are that you might get as good a deal here as good as in any other store. The selection doesn't rival the mega supermarket and isn't any way near as interesting as that pesented by the guy with the dog. This is the store that wants to kill the category killer, so the deals on national brands tend to be as good.

Let's look at some real life scenarios. The big box store has just been offered a scrumptious deal on a high profile Napa Valley Cabernet Sauvignon of an off vintage. They buy it all and stack it ten feet high and charge the unheard of price of fifteen bucks a bottle when it is regularly forty-five. Meanwhile the mahogany showcase wineshop across the street has just gotten their hands on five cases of the same wineries new release, best vintage cabernet at forty five dollars a bottle. This is a classic in wine dollar expendature management. Do you run amok with several friends and purchase many cases of the big box deal and suck it up on your porch while you and your buds wave the bottles and labels to passersby yelling that you bagged it for a steal. This is why big box stores sell so much wine.

Plan B- the more prudent wine buying course consists of taking a little time and researching the two vintages. That fifteen-dollar steal may wind up being a bomb that is worthy to be only drunk on your porch. That wine just across the street in the mahogany showcase may be the only five cases to make it into the state and may be the finest vintage of the decade, and may be a steal at forty five dollars a bottle. Hurry to both places. Do it fast. Both deals of this type and great vintages from the other guy don't last long. Buy a bottle of each and taste them immediately side by side and work on your plan. Just how good is that cheapie vintage? Have you tasted better for the money and is it still available? Also, just how good is that great vintage? Is it worth cellaring? Make the best decision for you economics, but remember- speed is of the essence here. You might want to buy a little of both. The everyday or weekend wine just to make you smile over what you have stashed away in your cellar. You can't sit on the porch deliberating over these decisions. Once you have your economics figured out go for it immediately.

Ironically, at the same time that the big box stores started offering expensive first growth Bordeaux stacked high up to the cieling in their hand made elegant wooden cases, right there next to the lawn furniture, just down the street Trader Joe was revolutionizing cheapness. A nameless someone in their company took to calling their dollar ninety-nine, cork finished, subtley labeled Charles Shaw brand Chardonnay and Merlot " Two Buck Chuck". Everyone gasped, and at a blink the rush was on. It was a consumer frenzy featured in all the national magazines, weekend news shows, and of course the wine writers were delirious. Eighteen million cases of "Two Buck Chuck" sold before the Bronco winery ran out. It was hailed as a classic in modern mob psychology and may wine up being on your MBA test.

The strange part of this phenonemon was that the wine didn't taste all that different from Bronco's standard everyday bag in the box wine at close to the same price. The major difference was the catchy, sexy appeal in getting something that was way cool for way cheap. Anyone could go out and buy a bag in the box wine, drag it into the old SUV and haul it home, but that seems just a bit tawdry. A couple of cases of "Chuck" on the other hand announce that you are a person of taste. Cheap taste, but taste nevertheless. The only problem with "extreme value" is that it does lead to extreme wine drinking boredom. Chuck is just a memory. If you want better flavors, just switch grape varieties frequently within the same price. Try sauvignon blanc instead of cherdonnay, or semillon for that matter. Also, with the reds do zinfandel, then switch to shiraz and onto cabernet.

When looking at all of the types of stores and their options you might want to look at trying this out. Your everyday wine can be shopped at the big boxes, or super chains, whoever has the best deals. The weekend wines, the ones of more interest that the guru can pair with food can be the mahogany showcase or the guy with the dog. Take some time seeking out the birthday and anniversary wines to get something interesting and unusual. Put the word out to your merchant about Thanksgiving, Christmas and New Years wines in early November. These should be your best wines of the year because afterall it is as much about the occasion as it is the wine. Ask your guru to save the most interesting wine that comes in and give you a call. Also, it is best to deal with the person who knows your likes and dislikes in selecting holiday wines. Spend a bit more than you intended because this is the time of the year when all the best stuff is released.

The most important thing in shop till you drop is not to get into a rut. Look for creative, imaniginitive wines in your budget.

There is always a hot new idea for a store. It will be something that is unique, stand on its own and is complete. There is a new breed of store featuring small selection, quite the opposite from the mega stores, and carefully selected wines not by label but by flavor. I call them the MTV stores as they lighten up the forboding verbage of countless computer generated tags and just keeps it simple. This is the For Dummies approach. Make it light and simple, removing all the pain and confusion. The jibberish of mindless winespeak incomprehensible beyond belief, is replaced with utter simplicity. In the new wine words, Vouvray becomes mellow yellow. The wine language is boiled down to exactly eight words, no meaningless signs, no winespeak, that no one in the store even knows what the taste is much less the ability to explain it to anyone. Our new words are: fuzzy, fresh, soft, luscious, juicy, smooth, big and sweet. They are placed as needed on 100 wine selections, and that's it. Wine minimalism. This is as simple as wine gets, and it is as refreshing as a cold glass of Vouvray (meke that mellow yello) But when you look at it, these words cover the types of wine that you will encounter. I would add only one, just for the overachieving winery, and that is complex. Shop 'till you drop all boils down to one thing-your style. It can be flamboyant, eccentric, cheap, expansive or creative. There are a mountain of wines to choose from out there, and many ways to choose them. In fact, some wines are even fizzy.

Restaurants:

Can't Live With 'em, Can't Live Without 'em

Restaurants as we know them today originated in France shortly after the Revolution in 1789. The nobility was dispatched, sometimes really dispatched, and their cooks, chefs, patissieres and countless assistants fled to Paris doing what they knew how to do best- cook. The newly enfanchized populace experienced in taste for the first time what it was like to be regal. They havn't been the same since. Restaurants sprouted up all over the planet using France food and wine as their model.

The big howling gripe from the consumers of wine mania since then has been the selection, service, storage and most importantly the prices restaurants charge for their wine. Just exactly why their markup has to be somewhere around three times cost is or should be if not a felony, at least a misdemenour. At least you get to experience a wide variety of the very good and the very bad in wines in restaurants. I suppose this is what keeps us coming back, the anticipation and the thrill of it all.

My alltime most frustrating wine experience in restaurants is that endured in most every fine sushi establishment. O.K., so there is absolutely no wine tradition in Japanese cuisine, but that never kept me or my trusty wholesale sales reps from draging in a variety of wines to taste with the staff, accompanied with a variety of adorable little table tents to put everywhere and the obligatory staff training to cap it all off. All ended with the same result. They stuck a small clip, about the size of a postit on their menu proudly announcing that they had saki, some Japanese beer, and if you were lucky a glass of the house chardonnay that came directly from the bag in the box out back.

This is dismal. Sushi is one of the alltime great culinary multi taste sensations on earth. Even sushi with training wheels (California rolls) are delicious. Even the ones with the stupid names that sound like drinks with little umbrellas are still good. Never have small dishes had more vitality: tuna, eel, octopus, calamari and salmon join the food elite of the world. And to wash it down with a six cent per ounce chardonnay verges on the ludicrous. I have cajoled, written pointed nasty articles, and resorted finally in desperation to takeout as a method of last resort. It beats the cheap saki, cheesy beer and six-cent chardonnay as the beverages of little choice.

I was guided by a friend to try a Japanese restaurant in Washington, D.C. as an alternative to the world of those little postits. Sushi Ko was billed as the great meeting of wine and sushi. We promptly booked a reservation and I ordered a glass of the essential beverage to have with sushi-Champagne. "Sorry, no Champagne" was the reply. So, I tried asking for a glass of chardonnay. They had only one or two, and those offered grudgingly. I then ordered up the wine list to see exactly what they did have in store. At least it was pages long and no postit. The lead question was on the inside cover page "Why Burgundy wines with Japanese foods"? Why indeed. I had never imagined such a thing. There was a little story about the owner and his great aunt and flower arranging ending with " the ultimate goal of our cuisine, like that of the art of ikebana (flower arranging) is to reveal the essence of each ingredient in its most honest and refined state." This is exciting and I haven't even opened the wine list yet.

We had been presented with a jaw dropping selection of fifty red Burgundies. Not only was this not a postit sized list, but these were the greats. The routine is simple, just order something by the glass to buy you some time with the list. It will enable you some time to dig out the vintage chart you carry and can examine the list more carefully. Red Burgundies, being the pinot noir grage are very vintage specific in quality. Burgundy is always about the place (that little hallowed spot of land), the pinot noir grape and the vintage. While having a little introductory bite of sushi and a glass of the house pour my task is to find the best vintage on the list (not necessarily the most expensive) and the one that has enough bottle age to really open up and dance. Usually 5 to 7 years in the bottle is perfect with Burgundy. Pair his with a little eel and some tuna, oh, and throw in some salmon and it is a memorable evening.

After an evening of the blissful flavors of sushi combined with a wine that has all the qualities of sweet cherries and wild mushrooms there is no going back to that pathetic postit list. If there isn't a Sushi Ko in your neighborhood, the absolute best that you can hope for is a decent bottle of bubbly, either Spanish, French or California and a good quality chardonnay as long as it doesn't come out of a box.

Sushi restaurants while a major problem aren't numerous enough to really be a wine nusiance. That has to fall in the eternal quest for a decent, interesting, unoxidized wine by the glass. While there is no wine tradition in Asian restaurants (give or take a few Vietnamese places that hung out with the French), there should be enough of a wine tradition in these United States to get a decent wine by the glass upon request. Mind you, the restaurant business has been a training ground for students working their way through college, and unfornately some have used the experience to fake their way through storage and service of wine. That is why, more likely than not, I shudder for a few moments before ordering a glass of wine.

There is, of course, the exception to the rule and this requires a visit to Philadelphia to the Panorama Ristorante. Fortunately, there is a little bed and breakfast upstairs so that you can crawl up to your hot tub after dinner with multi wine courses. The restaurant is a model for anyone interested in a serious lesson in wines by the glass. They cover quality, selection and just down right fascination. After years of flinching every time a glass is served in a restaurant, this place is a blessing and a relief.

Their wines are arranged in five wine flights of 1.5 ounces per wine. It is a tasting tour through all the world's lands of wine complete with whimsical titles attached. The big, full-bodied Italian Barolos and Barbarescos are called "Macho Mistos", and the little white wines of the nearby Pennsylvania region are termed "Local Yokels". It is a studied romp through the world of wine.

Little trips and flights are cool but backing all of this up is a 120-bottle cruvinet system pressurized with nitrogen. It's all fresh. These have to be among the 120 freshest glasses that you will ever encounter. You can then move on to a selection of three ounce tastes or the official five ounce glass, served up in oversized glassware. The most interesting flights to have are the ones titled "other". We are familiar with cabernet sauvignon, sauvignon blanc and chardonnr but to sit down eyeball to glass with tocai fruiliano, fiano and greco de tufo is wondrous stuff. These are grapes you have to go out of your way to find and try. Here you don't have to shell out for a bottle to experience them. The combined selection can run to 800 different combinations. They are kind about giving out their list so you can, when your taste buds are fatigued, do some of the combos in your head.

Unfortunately, the major overiding trend in restaurants is away from the fascinating and individual, those quirky brilliantly concieved winelists, but toward the corporate list that is well appointed, professional and executed with slight of hand. Since this represents an entire dining genre of many chains we won't splash names on the page. Lets have a look at what your credit card is buying these days.

The wine is the well-known Kendall Jackson Chardonnay. The distributor cost is from $10.00-11.00 and the restaurant price is $33.00. You have just left $23.00 of your money on the table. It is surprizing the back strip of your credit card didn't peel off during the transaction. The really sad part in all of this is that we observed a few pages back that the big box stores and category killers are selling this wine at cost or below. If only you can drag a little table with you into that category killer store and just cozy up with a little candle. K.J. chardonnay is one of the big wine centers of profit for Restaurant chains because they know you can't get along without it, and you can pronounce it. That little hint of oak and sweetness never hurt either.

Another of those slight of hand wines is the very sought after Sonoma Cutrer Russian River Ranches Chardonnay. Its distributor cost is $12.00 and the restaurant price is $49.00. This has always been a restaurant only wine that you can't find and compare in price at your big box store. Many a smart, smarmy, greedy restauranter makes a ton of money on this wine. Every time I order it in a restaurant I clench my teeth because I know that I have just left $37.00 on the table, and unfortunately you can't apply that toward the tip.

The sneakiest of all is when the winery offers a sizeable reduction to get their brand moving in the market. Such is the case with the very fine Oregon winery Torii Mor. They knocked their wholesale price down to $13.00 a bottle (a steal for that wine), and the restaurant chains in turn make it $66.00. Your server had better cut a fancy little act for that $53.00 in profit that you just threw onto the table. You can almost see them through the back of your head doing that little "bling bling" smile. Your only hope is to make a small restaurant list like the one that you made for the stores. Good wines like Bogle and Hogue, Ravenswood and Beringer can be had by the glass. They aren't high profile enough so that you can be indiscriminately gouged.

The thing that really amazes me about all of this is that people are more than willing to change the constitution to allow them to be shipped some little piss ant sweet wine that they had in Ohio but the restaurant solution is right under their noses. Each city could declare every Monday as BYOB night. You could bring your own bottle with no corkage fee or upcharge and leave part of that $53.00 as a tip. It wouldn't ruin the restauranteers profit, and it would encourage people to go out more often, especially if they weren't gouged up to their eyeballs in their wine prices. There is a tendency among progressive restaurants to take that markup down a bit. Lets face it, with not a lot of grand cellars full of inventory or sommeliers around these days the three times rule is wearing a bit thin. Fair prices should get you higher turnover. Now if only someone could convince the corporate chains of this.

The great restaurant search is for the place that is a wine maniac's destination. A place that you will gladly drive 300 miles to gaze at those thousand or so wines on a list. Destination lists are created by people with a single minded vision. People who can't wait for the chase, the capture and then the joy of stashing it into a cold, damp cellar. One of the best of these types of places is Park and Orchard in East Rutherford, New Jersey. Their list, aside from being great and all, is smothered with personal comments on both the wines and their cool times. You need to follow the same procejure here. Just order a glass of something red or white a bite and settle in to their list. The best course, and remember that glass of wine won't give you that much time, is to pick a section and go over it thoroughly.

My area of choice here is white Burgundy because of the depth of rarieties and their outstanding knowledge in this minefield of wines. Here you really need your vintage chart because they will have wines going back 15-20 years. The memory is good, it just isn't that good. Here is an instance where paying a premium really is getting a premium. To have all the greats from that small region laid out in front of you on several pages is miraculous. And they are all there.

You should get what you pay for in restaurants if you do a little homework. You can have wines by the glass, or look for the best priced bottles. Places like Spain, Chile and Argentina are exceptional values. If you know something about prices beforehand your chances are better. Don't be shy when you call for a reservation in inquiring about BYOB- you might just be surprized. The downside to all of this is leaving an extra $50.00 on the table for the opportunity of pressing your nose to the cork.

To Ship or not to Ship

"This is the best day for wine lovers since the invention

of the corkscrew" Clint Bolic, Institute For Justice Counsel

The maniacs, amateurs, nepotists, a couple of gurus and the entire

Latvia Syndrome itself have been struggling violently and long over whether

it should be legal to ship wine directly to consumers from one state to

another. Prior to now , half the states have permitted it, and half didn't. In

addition, there were also several conflicting constitutional points to gnaw

over- the commerce clause of the constitution versus the 21st amendment.

Blame it all on Al Capone. This little world affectionately known as the

three-tier system has mandated that the retailer buy from the wholesaler,

who in turn buys from the winery or importer. The Supreme Court just

altered this cozy system by a vote of 5to 4.

The citizen groups of the internet age have desperately been trying to

buy directly from the wineries of their choice even though it may or may not

save them money, or time, but in its own way has become a sexy thing to do.

Add a group of wineries who have wanted to ship to the public for as long as

they can remember, laying awake nights calculating all that extra profit in their heads. This is what can be refered to as a classic unconsumated relationship.

When we last left the wholesalers they still had tons of money, influence, political power and resolve. After all, this is their own pot of gold that these pesky internet types were attempting to take from them. The irony of the distributors is that they have had long periods of brilliance in protecting their lucrative franchise, or they could equally show flashes of pure nepotistic, opportunistic stupidity. In this particular case it is the latter. When confronted with the prospect of millions of Fed Ex, Ups, Postal Service, and God only knows what other carriers having packages full to the brim with wine not passing through their hands for their 30-40% cut- they choked.

The Washington Post on May 17th, 2005 reported that the distributors had formed a coalition comprized of both anti-alcoholism groups as well as The National Association of Evangelicals to stop the lockstep march of the small wineries and internet crazed wine shopping consumers. Their chronicled activities as a group should have been video taped for release on either Frontline or The Jerry Springer show, or made into a movie titled "The Really Odd Couple". What were the distributors thinking? Did these people ever meet or did they just conference call together?

Their primary defense against the possible change in the laws was to emphatically state that these parcels could possibly make it into the hands of young, under aged kids bent frantically on intercepting and consuming these delicious and exciting shipments. They missed only one element in their argument. Their well fininced whine would play well to the local PTA, but would hardly touch the justices of the Supreme Court. The underaged kids could perhaps bribe the garderner to go down to the corner store and purchase some cheesy kiwi/strawberry flavored malt beverage concoxion, which actually happens to be their favorite mindemenour elixier. Dad's bottles of cult Napa cabernet sauvignon aren't of the least interest to them So much for the nepotist distributor argument to protect our underaged citizens. It has been an argument that routinely hasn't convinced anyone. Little tidbits like providing orderly commerce, or tax collection or assisting the flow of goods make more sense. We pay cops to bust the gardiner, not the postman.

The real maniac group in this little drama is the consumers. They joined together as various groups such as "Save the Grapes" (and we know from what). The grapes that they really mean are the trophy kind, the wines that make it through their local nepotist distriburor in all too small a quantity, then get divided even further when they arrive at your local wineshop. We know the winery names: Abru, Arrowood, Beringer Sbragia, Bryant Family, Colgin, Dalla Valle, Dunn, Harlan, Kistler, Martinelli, Peter Michael, Shafer, Screaming Eagle, Silver Oak, Turley, Marcassin, and others. This is the pot of pure gold. The roadside stand, tourist wineries don't even enter into the equation as far as the collectors are concerned.

The most interesting statistic that has been bantied about is the fact that over 90% of wines in America are consumed within a few days of their purchase. Shipping wine to a consumer implies a particular type of consumer, or maybe it is one who doesn't live near a store, but I doubt it. Their argument is that they are creating a level playing field for all wines. This is a better argument than the nepotist distributors " junior's protection plan", but in actuality their personal vision is that of having a box seat in the owners section overlooking the great and famous Harlan Estate, with a glass and a corkscrew in their hands. Now, that is a level playing field!

The third group in this exciting drama of self interest is the wineries. There are thousands of them scattered throughout our land, but the one that has been doggedly determined to lead the shipping cause all the way to the supreme court is little Swedenburg Winery from Middleburg, Virginia.

When we last paid a visit to Virginia's wineries some 12 chapters and fifteen years ago they were all small and unorganized with few distributors interested in representing many of them. The thought here, and their plan, was that the tourist wine buying public would visit the winery in the bucolic countryside, and buy a tee shirt and some wine. They would then return to New York with a continual craving for this wine. Because of the anti-shipping laws the consumation of this vision didn't happen.

Juanita Swedenburg is suddenly all over the news, the 78-year-old poster person for small wineries. Standing erect with her tall stick stirring her little tank of wine, an American Gothic in a tasting room filled with the gee gaws of tourism. She is proof that there is a serious fact to all of the small wineries' distribution lamentations. The entire shipping controversy rests on the theory that wineries are not created equally. Distributors do pick and choose. We'll perform a little exercise to see how this works.

Open your phone book to Wine Distributors. Pick any one. You want to ask for the Sales Manager. Tell them that you are the National Sales Manager for Silver Oak Vineyards from Napa and that the local distributor is releasing the brand from their franchse. "Would you like to meet and talk?" Silver Oak is a pricy powerhouse at about $80.00 a bottle, with every bottle selling in minutes to the trophy wine people. The sales manager, without a doubt, will drop everything and meet with you in fifteen minutes with a contract drawn up.

Our second brand that we will use to call a distributor is Adelsheim Vineyards. They are a small, highly touted winery in the Willamette Valley in Oregon .Ironically, this brand sells well locally with distributors, out of the tasting room in Newberg, Oregon and they are proponents of direct shipping as well. Your distributor sales manager will not be as quick to act on this one, they will have to check with their reps in the field and call a few stores and restaurants. In about an hour or so you will receive a return call and they will meet tomorrow with the papers all drawn up. Not quite the slam dunk of Silver Oak, but good nonetheless.

The theory here is that there is always a strong need for high quality pinot noir and pinot gris in the market and Adelsheim is written up frequently by the wine press, both local and national. This brand will add to the portfolio and fill in where there are needs. It will take a little building, but both the winery and distributor will benefit.

Our third call is from the Sweedenbourg Winery of Middleburg, Virginia. It faces the same immediate reluctance as Adelsheim but none of their contacts have ever heard of them. There is nothing in the wine magazines and nothing in The Oxford Companion to the Wines of North

America (one of the few books that lists Virginia wine). This is not looking good. When the sales manager calls back, they state that after checking with stores and restaurants, there is no demand for the wine in the market. Unfortunately, transferring the tee shirt buying crowd from the tasting room into a brand that sells off the shelf of a store takes lots of press and thousands of miles of sales calls by those reps in their funky cars.

The major problem for small wineries is that 50 states have them and only four states wines have any real renown beyond their local tasting rooms: California, Washington, Oregon and New York. The notion of shipping has wide appeal because the chances of breaking out of tee shirt land aren't great. Our little scenario with the distributor is not far fetched. I have been on all sides of that phone call and have seen it played out countless times. Wine mania does not get its name for nothing.

It is true as the "save the grapes" people and their allies maintain, the playing field is far from level as it stands today, and is also pretty bumpy as well. Distributors and their fellow wineries control to a large extent where wines go and how they sell. The best way for a winery to break loose from their everyday life and to completely reinvent themselves is to become part of something quite larger that themselves. Ravenswood started life as a small California zinfandel producer with iconic crows on its label. They made some very good wine and had a strong following. They were wines that people wanted. They were wines that Constellation wanted.

Constellation (reinvented itself from Canandagua of Wild Irish Rose fame) was determined to become a giant in winery ownership at all levels of size. They purchased Ravenswood with the idea of taking them from the restaurant world, purchasing a whole lot of grapes, and taking them to that magic world called " the next level ". Ravenswood is currently stacked to the ceiling in big box stores throughout the country. Smaller brands aren't shoved aside, they are dumped aside. The big box stores, the big brands and their owners are living their own sets of lives with consumers.

The battle has been pitched between the free trade "ship me those trophy wines now" group and the distributors, a power entity unto themselves. There have been countless tens of thousands of pages written and there will be many more after it is all done. Having run a small winery, been in both sales and management for both small and large distributors, and having bought for retailers, I can guarantee one thing. All those little Juanita Swedenburg sized wineries of middling interest that are barely known and are off the beaten path probably won't ship all that much wine to out of state consumers. The wineries that will clean up in this little sweepstakes will be the trophy wines. The small wineries that are already distributed and receive good reviews, like Adelsheim, should do well in shipping if their prices are fair and the shipping is reasonable. Just another comparison chart for you to prepare. And having done a bit of comparison, winery prices will differ enormously.

The most curious part of this long, painful, expensive exercise in democracy is the big what If? With the current consolidation taking place in all of wine mania the large, and getting larger big box wine retailers have to be thinking of bypassing the distributors as well. If the consumer is purchasing wine direct from the out of state winery of their choice then why can't retailers do the same. What is to keep that big box stack of Ravenswood from coming direct from the winery in the future? And while we are at it, why can't every other store display come direct from the source, shrinking the selection of stores and restaurants down considerably. Also, those direct winery prices may or may not be a great deal for the internet consumer. As we witnessed in the 1990's your favorite little winery when fueled with sufficient amounts of press can go completely over the top in price, and there is, after all ,a 40% distributor profit just sitting there like a fat pile of unused money on the table . The theory behind shipping direct was one of increased access and lower prices. Actuality can always be something a little different.

Wine mania doesn't often reveal the blatant life of self interest as it has in this case. Every single group, and there have been lots, has been interested in their own outcome with no concern over what would happen to everyone else. As the New York Times reported on Dec. 11, 2002 Juanita Swedenborg said if she had been allowed since 1988 to ship wine direct to New York that she would have sold maybe 300 cases. That comes to a whopping 21 cases a year. Wine mania is smaller than we thought. Also, one of those nepotistic distributors could have easily taken on a dark horse like Juanita, but now the empire that dad built is on the verge of a several billion dollar overhaul. And guess who is going to get overhauled? The distributors, plus the medium to smaller sized stores could vanish as the gigantic big box stores will either purchase direct from the winery, or create their own labels. The selection could dramatically decrease locally, unless, of course you wish to have your own wine shipped to you, which is kind of where we started in the first place. There will be years of shakeout in this little drama, with the lawyers filling their cellars to the brim- with trophy wines, of course.

The 60 Days of Wine Mania

This is it. The 60 days that the wine maniacs both live for and dread. During the months of November and December all winedrinkers, frequent, seldom and barely ever at all, come out at once. This is a chaotic blend of wisdom, incompetence and sheer chaos all jammed into 60 glorious days. Essentially wine mania is not large enough to handle all of this- all of them in this compressed duration. The stores, even the largest, are not all that big in light of the enormous upsurge in traffic.

The worst are the utterly confused semi-wine drinkers. They magnify the confusion. They don't exactly know what that wine was that they had in San Juan five years ago, but it is their favorite, and yes, it comes in a blue bottle. Does that help? Immensely. This is the vast majority of people who drop what they have been doing and drop in on the 60 days of wine mania. The best occurance is that we have them all in front of us on our turf. Wine to us is one thing, having it with food and living what Robert Mondavi calls the "good life"- good wines surrounded with family.

The 60 days of wine mania reach three distinct fever pitches, all different in their own way: Thanksgiving, Christmas and New Years.

Thanksgiving is by far the scariest, what with all of those relatives, and all of those dishes (what does go with brussel sprouts), and all those wines, and the turkey, we can't forget the turkey. The irony is that if you pick up any half-baked food and wine mag during November all of that stuff will be revealed. That was too easy.

Everyone in wine mania, from the wineries, distributors, restaurants and retailers, has been eagerly awaiting this moment (some less eager than others) and is armed with all of the answers to the best of their ability. Speaking as one who has worn a wide variety of the hats of the 60 days of wine mania that the only yawner is being the press. You can't imagine the excruciating boredom of trotting out the same tired old wine and food groups every year. The names may change but if you look at say a half dozen food mags, everything is virtually identical.

Several organizations need to step forward to enlighten the huddled Thanksgiving masses. Small wineries in all regions of the US could take out ads pairing their wines with the giblets or could print up little turkey designs of bottle neckers to hang from their Thanksgiving friendly wines. All of Alsace, France, its length of 70 miles by 2 miles wide could benefit and be benefitted as a land growing Thanksgiving wines. It is time that they became enlightened by having their entire region run ads and ply articles from the winewriters telling of the compatability with Alsace and the bird. The great thing about Alsace and small US wineries is that they make it so easy. A single grape name on the label with a brand, and that's it. This would be a Thanksgiving miracle if the middle aged couple from Kansas strolled into the wine store of their choice and automatically ordered up some Trimbach Pinot Gris for the bird. No panic, no worry, no fuss.

There are several other groups that could jump on the Thanksgiving bandwagon. The 3rd Thursday in November, the arrival of the Beaujolais Nouveau once a gigantic occasion has whimpered down several notches. Now, Nouveau Beaujolais just happens to be one of the alltime great Thanksgiving wines. This stuff even works with the brussell sprouts. Maybe those cashflow laden producers could come up with all manner of point of sale with birds and nouveau, and even a few sprouts. This is also really good stuff to taste out with the mostly seldom if ever wine drinking public. It has all that slurpy, grapey, just out of the vat flavor. It won't scare anyone.

The big winners could very well be the Zinfandel producers. They resemble more a political party than a mere grouping of California wine producers. They make red and pink colored wines. Their main fan group ZAP (Zinfandel Advocates and Producers) rose in ten years from a tasting under the tent organization to a football stadium sized throng not afraid to shell out their money and their time to taste their faves and a couple of hundred unknowns as well. Zinfandel, in case you havn't noticed, goes great with turkey, and gravey and giblits as well. Maybe the red zin people and the white zin people could talk and hire the best car painter and designer to cover a NASCAR car from head to toe. Its not as if they havn't made enough from the blood of the grape to afford this supposed indulgence. Especially the red grape turned pink.

ZAP needs to get on the ball and do zin billboards, zin mousepads, zin aprons, zin everything. Their campaign slogan could be "With the bird, just say zin". Just think of all those Kansans walking in and saying "Just a bottle of zin, please". Thanksgiving would be a better place in wine mania with just a few of these wine types imbeded into the cerebral cortex of a few million Americans.

Also, if the zin producers are exceptionally smart, they will introduce the public at large onto the fact that zinfandel, not only cabernet sauvignon, is a wine that makes vintages that are worthy of their attention as well. The hardened, crazed, stand in line for weeks ZAP people are aware of this fact, but the gen(eral) pub(lic) wouldn't know a superior vintage of zinfandel if it turned into the Thanksgiving turkey.

Christmas is different because you actually have an older wine tradition lurking in the wings for this, the second of our wine mania holidays. The wines that you completely forgot about actually exist: Lancers, Blue Nun, Mateus, Cherry Kjiafa, and the cheap madieras for basting things. The wines of a bye gone era. In fact, they could all get together and run a promotion with, say, a Thomas Nast Santa Claus as their spoksperson, with his outfit a little frayed and discheveled.

The other group of wine maniac producers who could grab ahold of the 60 days of wine mania are the riesling producers. They are always threatening to meke a spectacular comeback and maybe unseat chardonnay from its throne, and they don't. Their forte, and they don't have a clue is ham. As traditional a Christmas dish as exists and this unbelievable large group of potential admirers waiting to just grab hold of that blue bottle and let it rip into those tiny glasses. Riesling, and how hard is that to remember or pronounce. Put a riesling label atop every ham in the US. Billboards with ham and its natural accompaniment, why riesling, of course.

This would be a giant step toward escaping from the clutches of the Latvia Syndrome. Since the rieslings will be going to screw caps, there isn't a bit of worry about that one bottle a year non -cork screw owning group (and it is vast) not drinking any wine. They will be yours.

The last group to get together will poney up their funds to do major television commercials. These are the shiraz producers. They have been sensational on their own without even dipping as much as a cork into the untapped Latvia Syndrome ocean. The wine is luscious, juicy, and generally has that little hint of cola flavor that we all either love or remember.

The entire idea behind this little exercise is that wine mania should exist as a delirous art form far beyond the 60 days of wine mania, when they all go back to their cacoons and disappear for the next 305 days. Everyone in the biz runs like crazy, gets extremely giddy, then they are gone. It is all over. Wine can and should become a modicum of part of our lifestyle, instead of in its present form as an exercise in stupidity carried out by the majority of the population. Learning about and using wine is far easier than learning about rocket science, but too many people still thing that this isn't the case.

The way for all of this to become real is for the winery groups to get together. The Alsatian families have been coming to the US for decades. It isn't far fetched for all of them to coop a budget and go for a pairing with the bird for Thanksgiving. Likewise with the zinfandel people, as the grape doesn't cost lots of money compared with others out there, and the American oak cooperage is reasonable. They could bombard the entire heartland with full color turkey ads and lots of bottles of zin. The riesling producers with fairly high yield and no oak aging should be able to cozy up to those hams via magazine ads in all the zillions of food and wine publications. The Champagne producers did it for the Milennium and havn't been seen since. That is unfortunate, for us as well as for them.

The shiraz people have all the clout going for them right now. They have all those cute names that everyone can memorize, the penguins, koalas, and not to mention a bevy of household pets. The shiraz people as a group could make it happen. The foods that you traditionally know, paired with the wines that are both tasty and easy to remember. If that doesn't get us another hundred days of Latvia Sindrome people climbing aboard, then I don't know what will. The only time that you see these people is during the 60 days, and believe me, you get them as afraid and huddled masses. They are scared to death of the mysterious subject known as wine. It is the people who are into it who are mystified, the others are just plain scared. Relieve them of their fear and wine mania will be another place altogether.

Afterword from the Wine Maniac

The one truism in wine mania is that we are either patting ourselves heartily on the back, or are freaking out. With our Latvia sized per capita consumption it is easy to grin over our small victories. America is still weighing in at between 2 and 2.4 gallons of wine per person YEARLY. The soft drink people snicker over their 54 gallons per person, and even the coffee people can gloat at theirs at 30. The French and the Italians are still weighing in at 16 gallons of wine….each. Looks like nothing has changed. Actually, it has, on the inside, in our collective brains. Wine is available and accepted throughout America, still we just don't drink that much of it.

California has Risen: California went in a few short years from winning the Paris tasting with a few hundred wineries just hanging around, to having wine as a part of their permanent lifestyle. From eccentric local farmers to global players, this place has led with technology, creative tastes and a searing drive to win big that is part of living in the Golden State.

Through the tasting of the ordinary, the interesting, and the trophy wines I still miss funky guys like Nervo on the scene. The work of the deliberate peasant brings uniqueness to the table. It is a uniqueness that the wine executives of both globalization and its more local form gobbilazition (the eating and digesting of local wineries) can't duplicate. It is because their calculator is always blocking the view of their wineglass. California needs just a light to moderate sprinkling of deliberate peasants on what can become no more than a delightful confection.

Later Oregon: The color of wine in Oregon has grown bright from pinot noir. They have created a lighter palate than California. This place is exciting because no one saw them coming. Oregon is now awash in wineries. The newer people are different, they aren't amateurs or nepotists but are equal to the task of being wine maniacs. I call them career regifters. They had a success the first time around and are fashioning their wineries to reflect their original image. They know exactly who they are.

Every time I taste Oregon wine, and that is often, they still have their own uniqueness of flavor. They want to be Burgundy so badly but they don't have the nerve to admit it, even when they whip up on the French in a tasting. The Oregon single vineyard worshipfulness can get overly pricey, but they are still wise enough to dance around their tasting rooms with calculator in hand until they get it right. They usually wind up getting it right.

I don't know how this or the Early Oregon chapter will be received there. They may hate it because the career regifters are doing a whole lot of myth making with their founding fathers. There are a host of mags, newspapers and books from the 1970's if they would care to do some checking. Wine is as much a lifestyle in Oregon as in Europe so the local wine maniac will be protective and cautious of their stories and myths. Every emerging wine region needs to send some emmisaries to this place and see just how both the making and the local fanaticism of wine should be done.

Big Sky Country: Two wineries sprung up in Montana. That doesn't look like much at first glance, but when you consider that the wind chill gets to –50 degrees, this is a colossal act of faith in wine mania. The Campbells, Pere and Fils have been growing riesling in Kalispell for 15 years or so. You need to visit on the 4th of July when they have the fabulous pow wow in Arlee just down the road. The mountains, the indians, the wine, this is the Montana experience.

Earl, the man who wears the boots made from many of God's creatures wrested the Gallo brand from golf cart boy, otherwise things are pretty much the same.

On My Own in France: This is the most glowingly romantic experience, and the toughest work. Nothing is harder than being chilled to the bone in those cellars. You know at the time that this is way cool, but that your body temperature has just dropped toward the danger zone.

No one knows the wines of their own zip code better that the French. They now have the interest to taste all the world's wines, and believe it or not recently I have tasted some Australian style lookalike wines made by the French themselves on their very own turf. Don't go there boys. It isn't worth trading a few zillion cases of sales today in exchange for the miracles of those growers in Chablis, Bordeaux, the Loire, Burgundy, and others too numerous to mention.

Virginia Wines: Form and Substance: Like Oregon, Virginia wines have changed dramatically. Mainly, there are more of them. They are better than they were 15 years ago, but they still need that giant boost of both quality and recognition. Too many are still mired in that other worldly tourist industry that is Virginia. "Would you care for a tee shirt with that bottle of wine?" Fortunately, there are two gurus who are usually listened to by the wineries. Dr. Tony Wolfe on vines and Dr. Bruce Zoechlin on wines.

There are still some nasties that have multiplied. Too many different wines are made by most wineries. Is 35 too many? Yes. And when the words quality control are spoken, we are not speaking in tongues. There has to be a system to test and varify quality, and alert the winery about their lack thereof. The national press needs to be made aware of the best of this state's wines, and not just through the rumor of some peeved consumers gag reflex.

The Paris tasting should be on every grape grower's mind every day. You first knock somebody off their pedistal, then get out of your tasting rooms and see what the real world is about. You can do it. You just have to want to do it.

Gigantic Wine Distributor: Recently, a local grocery chain has put the pedal to their wine medal and the GWD (gigantic wine distributor) has gotten just that much bigger. There has, of course, been a change in local and state politicos, but that hasn't changed contributions, backslapping or promises at bit. The Semi-Jim has grown larger too, and so has his car.

Lots of extreme value varietals have been added, not many local or regional wines, as one would hope. There have been a host of Koala bear, Kangaroo and penguin wines, and for the Christmas holidays the Blue Suede Elvis Chardonnay, Jailhouse Merlot, and Elvis the King Cabernet. The holiday piece de resistance is Le Snoot, four labels featuring four varieties of wines, each with fashionably attired cartoon pigs holding tiny wineglasses. Nice touch. I really do wonder what ever happened to Jogging in a Jug?

Wine buyer from Hell: You do all of that wine scouting and buying for three essential kinds of wine purchasers that comprize the wine buying public. The first, and by far the most common, is the person who wants a bottle to accompany tonight's dinner. This is the vast majority of wine drinkers, irrespective of how much they know or what they are willing to spend on that bottle.

The second is a person who has a "cellar". This can range from a twelve bottle plug in temperature control box sitting over the fridge to a massive 5,000 bottle room outfitted as cellar, cave and shrine, all at the same time. Their duty to the shrine and the wines inside is to faithfully log everything in and out and to record the changes in nuances of flavor each time a bottle of the precious cargo is consumed. Reading up on the subject is a necessity and having multiple hobbies frowned upon, lest you miss an exciting purchase. It is easy to fake your way through this hobby, because what is one persons bread box is another persons shrine.

The third is, of course, the true collector. I have been fortunate to appraise several major collections that were staggering in depth, quality and money expended. The true collector has the money of Croesis, the reflexes and speed of a cheeta, the patience of Job in not to open their treasure too quickly, and the stealth of a commando. Forget playing golf because a rare treasure may be sold while you are lounging on the 7th hole. Most important, the collector specializes in the greats in wine, and only in the finest vintages. The size of the collection matters less than the unattainability and greatness of the wines. Record everything just like the provenance of any other great work of art.

Live on the Radio: There should be somewhere in the radio world either a Click and Clack wine talk show where we'll fix up your vinous problems or a late night insomnia style program with both chef and wine person in the booth together ranting and raving into the way early A.M. There could also be a good drive time wine show to get your taste buds going. If the chef is there for drive time you might actually return home with a good recipe, a wine combination and a bottle of something interesting. There is a real need in radio land for shows. God knows, I have done my part.

Local Wine Journalist: The number of local wine journalists is shrinking. At the same time there are exactly one zillion new specialty magazines springing up. You shouldn't have to get your wine information from just one or two major sources. You could join a wine chat room, but you might as well be chatting with yourself.

We are the Judge and Jury: I have always enjoyed when people walk up to me after a competition and ask why I voted for so and so wine. Judges usually bring their notes to the press conference and can fill you in to their thoughts and their votes. The smart way is to ask about why you gave either no medal, bronze and silver, not just the gold. There are wine competitions all over the U.S. So few people take advantage of this, and after all we don't growl or bite, in case you were wondering. Show up, ask and compare.

Teacher with a Glass: The wine class is still going strong. It is humorous how many ex-students that I run into who have taken up a lifelong interest in wine. This is still the best way to start learning about the subject. Find the nearest University class and just take it. O.K.?

Wine and Food Culture: Try not to have the same wine twice, get out there and experiment. Try to pair a wine with dinner as frequently as you can. When dining out, ask the waiter for their recommendation, and make sure that it isn't a wine that you have had before. There are a handful of writers on food and wine who have a first rate book on wine and food in print all of the time. Andrea Immer is both good and prolific. Linda Johnson Bell has Pairing Wine and Food, and we all hope that this one never goes out of print before our copies fall apart. Joanna Simon is also terrific. Red wine with Fish by the boys is well out of print and has been for years. It is pricy on e-Bay but is worth it. Wine and food pairing is about the more experience you have, the better you become. It is your path to guruness in a glass.

Finding Great Wine Dinners: Pick up the paper and get on top restaurants e-mail lists. They haven't slowed down a bit. Not a bad idea to pick your favorite themes and go to those dinners.

Cork Dorks, Scroogies and the Rest: Funny how these things happen. There are more screw caps emerging lately- everywhere. Have you noticed?

60 Days of Wine Mania: Here it is at the end of January and everything is qiuet. Too quiet. All the wine consumers have gone away as they do every year to emerge again in either the spring or the fall, depending upon their confidence level. Some day everyone in wine mania will kick on the holiday afterburners and we will catch up with Argentina in consumption.

The Maniacs Adjourn: choose the best vintages from the top winemakers for the most important occasions and drink the remainder on Tuesday or Wednesday night.And don't forget to work on your own set of wine maniac stories. Wine still conveys deep symbolic importance whether it is for a wedding or the most profound religious event. It has always conveyed magic to civilization. That is largely what propels the wine maniac forward, to be part of something that is much bigger that himself.

There are not a lot of things in this life of wine mania that I would change, just things that I would have probably done more of. The radio show was a Saturday lark but in retrospect it was unique. After listening to a few tapes I should have quit my day job, found a large sponsor, and gone for it.

The other thing is the one on one interview with the wine guru that you pursue as a journalist. I want to do more of them. Whether attending the classic chumps night out dinner, or a two hundred winery tasting of ZAP you come away with grand flavors, but not a whole lot of in depth of information. The one on one interview is an energizing event. Any time that you have an opportunity to read one, you need to do it.

I did get that interview with Robert Mondavi and asked him my most perplexing question- why must we be doomed to live with the Latvia Syndrome? He wisely answered " The wine industry has done a poor job of marketing. The large wineries are afraid. There have to be wine and food programs in the universities. There has never been any alcohol abuse in my family because we view wine as a food. Students need to be educated about wine. Everything (should be) in moderation."

So there you have it. A life in wine mania. If there is a moral to this strange little adventure, it is don't be afraid to go out and try something new. Buy a good wine book or two, take a class, read a good wine magazine, and record the wines that you taste. The best thing about wine mania is that it can be new, fresh and fulfilling for a lifetime.